To Ian & Moira
love, Lu Wailu

John Wendon

LEE WAISLER

THE ART OF
LEE WAISLER

JOHN WENDON

ANDRE DEUTSCH

First published 1990 by
André Deutsch Limited
105-106 Great Russell Street
London WC1B 3LJ

British Library Cataloguing in Publication Data
Wendon, John
  The art of Lee Waisler.
  1. American visual arts
  I. Title
  709.2

  ISBN 0 233 98612 X

Printed in Singapore by Kim Hup Lee Printing Co Pte Ltd

FILAMENT SUNS
over greyblack desolation.
An idea
tall as a tree
takes on the resonance of light: there are
songs yet to be sung on the far side
of mankind.

IN THE SNAKE TUNBRIL, past
the white cypress,
through the flood
they drove you.

Yet in you, from
birth,
the other wellspring was foaming,
in remembrance
of blackest light
you clambered to the day.

from *ATEMWENDE* (1967)
poems by Paul Celan
translation John Wendon

CONTENTS

The Language of an Artist
1

Notes to the Illustrations
25

'Point of Departure' by Lee Waisler
40

Plates
41

List of Illustrations
89

THE LANGUAGE OF AN ARTIST

Like music, visual art communicates in its own language. Like verbal language, it has its syntax (forms), its rhetoric (aesthetics) and the style by which the personal signature of the artist is identified.

It does not, however, have a specific vocabulary of meaning outside its own frame of reference, except in so far as it may subscribe to historically recognised artistic conventions or iconographies.

In modern art especially the emphasis is on the artist's own, singular contribution to meaning, achieved in a critically individual blend of line, form, colour, pattern and space. Therein lies the heart of its matter: that it creates the language in which it seeks to be understood. Verbal communication expresses consciousness, but visual language is capable of being not only an act of pre-lingual perception but can be about consciousness itself. It prescribes not so much what we see but how we may see it.

The first order of communication therefore lies with the work of art itself. At any level, an attempt at introducing an artist in the language of words should always be subject to the caveat that a work of art creates its own ambience and ideally demands an untranslated response. That is paramount.

But by the same token there is the shock of innovation: the viewer needs to recast his understanding and his eye to the new language, and that effort may not always immediately yield results without some model or introduction, bearing in mind the freshness of vision and the possible opaqueness in meaning which a work may at first have for us.

We who are not artists, are not native to the new. We depend for our visual vocabulary on what we have seen before. In coming to terms with the idiom of an innovative artist at first acquaintance we can expect, therefore, some sense of obtuseness, as well as maybe curiosity and excitement. But then, if the new work has the power, we seek to share in its truth. The present comments are about sharing truth with one artist, in words which claim to be only a lattice, shaped to their subject approximately.

INFLUENCES

Locating an artist on the map of his time is a first step to sharing his work. The important, personal coordinates for Lee Waisler are that he was born in California in 1938 to a Jewish family who had reached California from central Europe. He has practised art since his young manhood. He has a studio in Los Angeles and another in Holland. He is widely read in many fields: poetry, psychology, the religions, iconographies and modern art. He carries such learning lightly and there is about him a robust and spontaneous energy which day by day invigorates his outlook.

He was raised into what one might describe as a protestant-Jewish tradition, that is one in which rabbinical influence was fading and in which Jewish culture and conscience has become internalised. Waisler lives the Jewish encounter with an inexplicable hidden God, outside the synagogue, as a universal encounter. He finds that the temple is empty, its columns fissured and that there can be no mediator. It is a more taxing and a more lonely quest.

1

Blended to Waisler's Jewish conscience is his consciousness of his place under the Californian sun, with its ancient, native geological identity, its absorption of the world's cultures and professed command of the material earth and its untrammelled instinct for extending the frontiers of man. A prime focus for him is the reconciliaton of nature and man in this amazingly rich but finite environment. One cannot help but think of Waisler the artist as a man with a central European imagination as his divining rod, dowsing for man's spirit in the Californian soil. Like all of us, he is a native of his land, in search of home.

For landmarks, Waisler takes his bearings from the events of Western historical experience in the last 100 years.

I. The central feature is the post-Nietzschean heritage of the death of God and the acknowledged burden of having to fill that loss with the godlike consciousness of the artist: a dilemma of awesome seriousness and paradox, with the order of the created world subverted by man's own creativity. The more God has receded from men's awareness the more prominent and urgent the fiat of the artist in filling the spaces of sensibility left vacant in a deistic and salvational universe. The effects of freedom and of desolation were one and the same; who could breathe the thin air of an abandoned dispensation? As God fell silent, what was for man, the artist, to say? Everything was possible; anything was lawful — but where was the location of meaning?

As dislocated forms swirled about the head of the artist, birth was given to abstract art — the consolations of chaos, broken narrative, fragmented figures of humanity, games with perception, lines and colour in a play of pattern for its own sake, hints of innocence and of experience unanchored except in the fathomless deep of incoherent (un)consciousness, such were the targets for the visual artist. Among the finest, most wide-ranging and most interesting for Waisler were Klee and Duchamp.

II. The intellectual and moral debris of man's catastrophe in losing God was flung into the historically equivalent catastrophe of the First World War. Waisler has absorbed the work of the Russian constructivists and suckled on the wizened breasts of post-war German expressionism, with its penchant for angry irony and its capacity for venting bankrupt aesthetic reaction to express the shock of a culture in a moral vacuum. European Expressionism marked the terminus of agreeable aesthetics; the consensus of form was comprehensively destroyed upon the easels of the artist as an ironic hero of void creation.

III. The genocide of Jews during the Hitler period was the hinge of horror which closed the door upon all regenerative norms drawn from historical

2

experience. No Jew who survived (and who, in the face of that unique crime, is not a Jew? It was done to all, for all generations) has been able to live a moral life without the continuum of that suffering in the holocaust suffusing all other perspectives, including not least the perspectives of art. That wound, unlike all other wounds, bar the one inflicted upon another Jew two millennia before, will never heal. For a Jewish artist certainly it will always suppurate from his work in symbols of inconsolable pain. In mimesis, the deathly path trodden by the perpetrators and their victims will appear again and again, like a prayer, in the etchings and canvases of Lee Waisler; and not only in those specifically dedicated to the subject, such as *The Most Travelled Road* from the series entitled *Homage to Primo Levi* (in the Yad Vashem in Israel), but also in the *Stone Oath* group of paintings and in others.

3 DAYS OF VIGIL

THE NIGHT HELD UGLY SURPRISES

4

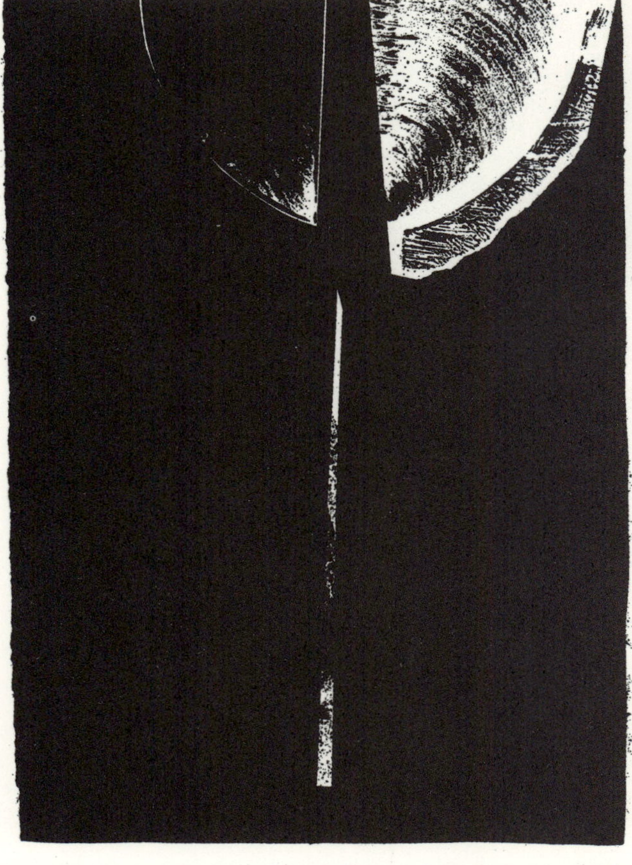

5 A HARD VOICE

How will a Jewish artist find expression today for the holocaust wound? Waisler offers his answer to that question in the germinal black which is the ground of nearly all of his canvases, in the abstract expressionist figures of skeletal emblems and in the tentative altars for a waiting devotion — see the *Gnomon* paintings — upon which so many of the canvases are centred, and then raimented like a darkly glowing fire — the furnaces of the holocaust will never die down — fed by the jewels of humanity burning, in colours of an inexpressively rich conflagration. Two quite pre-eminent canvases call to be mentioned in this context: *What Is To Be Remembered* and the very recent *Blood Libel.* The latter has moved on from the fires and back to the unextinguished, recurrent pain of unfounded hate.

IV. Those who stepped away from the Second World War on the winning side were at once confronted/affronted by the paradox of their power: the atom bomb. The world's security and overall peace appeared to be poised on the tip of the most awesomely destructive weapon ever invented and entrusted to the hands of political weathervanes!

In the late 1960s Waisler responded by putting his aesthetics in the service of a cause. The state, in pre-war Germany, had proved to be an organised crime: if that could be, then no state could be trusted. The public, in whom the state had an interest only as a docile, regimented source of social energy, needed to be challenged by the conscience-fingering of anarchy and outrage. Protest and art in symbiosis could shock communities into change of political course. Street events were not only for the volatile crowd but for the rhetoric of art. Art could have a voice, a social, public meaning. Upon this conviction, Waisler founded a number of ventures in support of peace and social justice. The most long-lasting and indeed the most compelling of these was his outdoor, mobile sculpture, *Under the Mushroom* (first displayed at the US and Soviet Embassies in Holland in 1978 and then taken to atomic test sites and campuses in the US). It remains an active black presence on many a public occasion; most recently in Italy. But by now even *Under the Mushroom* has official approval; mayors and civic dignitaries like to be seen in its

6

7

8

shadow! It is, however, a reminder that the artist, Lee Waisler, will be ready always to go into public places with brush and paint to do battle in the causes of life, profoundly suspecting public abuses of power and alarmed by the clouds of death spreading across the earth at the hands of expedient materialism. In 1987 the eminent Italian art historian Arturo Schwarz wrote of Waisler as follows:

> '. . . I respect both the man and the artist . . . he has the courage of his own convictions and is not afraid of committing himself, even politically . . . Remaining faithful to his inner model, he gives us a work of robust elegance, heart-rending purity and balanced harmony.'

It should, however, also be understood that it is of the essence of Waisler's public involvements that the rhetoric always remains subordinated to aesthetic purity and harmony in his work. An interesting example of this is a specifically public set of sculptures which is still in the form of maquettes, waiting for realization on a very large scale appropriate for a town square. Each massive black rectilinear block in steel or stone creates in a particularly pure form a focussed relationship to the small-scale human being who, the artist conceives, should approach the sculpture below its base from an underground passage in order to stand directly at its centre. The sculpture thus becomes a monument to the individuality of the human spectator/participant. The conception is of a contrast in masses which points not to the obliteration of the human being by the scale of the steel or stone block but to his protection or recognition under it.

V. One very powerful American response to the paradoxes of post-war artistic awareness was to shed load: the abstract expressionists, like Kline, de Kooning, Still, Pollock and Rothko adopted an ostentatiously non-historical 'vernacular' which, in the setting of the antecedent work of artists profoundly aware of the paradoxes of all artistic statements, was provocatively illiterate. The work of the abstract expressionists entailed the deconstruction of or a withdrawal from elaborated pictorial communication, figurative statement and the accumulated metaphorical paraphernalia of the historical schools. By the size, vigour and daring of the canvases the abstract expressionists not only appeared to throw off the self-consciousness inherent in artistic awareness but to engage the elementals of paint and colour as a weapon, in disregard for graphic or sculpted form or function or reference or organisation. These artists did not mediate or profess to metamorphose existing forms or realities: their canvases created spaces; spaces which were there to evoke the responses of the viewer and which had a power to move or to disturb.

As the options available to perception and response accordingly contracted, the exploration of certain specific visual singularities such as colour, line, fabric, texture, tonalities was brought to the forefront and enormously enlarged in a bold attempt by the abstract expressionists to objectify the qualities of perception for these bare elements of visual presentation. In turning their face against figurative statements, they achieved in their most successful work an energetic austerity which in turn could open the way to a very important fresh access of feeling.

While the early 'language' of the abstract expressionists was a limited metalanguage about the artist and his materials, their later work, and especially that of Rothko and Still, became less reductive and more persuasive. It let in emotion. In the presence of a late Rothko canvas one is in a self-defining space comparable to the effect to be drawn from the windows of a Gothic cathedral or the light in a mosque; his spaces breathe with a like elation. But they do not express or depend upon articulated belief. On the contrary, they are without thematic focus and, either being without reference to anything beyond themselves or invoking a bare spectrum of feeling, they are on the yonder side of meaning somewhere in the realm where mysticism might have its beginning. The spectator will look in vain for reference and it is questionable whether these canvases are anchored in any kind of reality outside their own created dream. Their beauty is the equivalent of 'sound' music: an idiom without voice.

One may sense Waisler's debt to this American school in the heroic size of some of his canvases and in his feel for the transformational power of his medium — colour, sand, glass, wood, canvas. His materials are made to speak with their own intense creativity; the secret is that they are transformed into fields of energy.

But Waisler in his achievement has moved on, past abstract expressionism's cultivated incoherence. He is an imagist and he works in a visual language which is intent on artistic meaning. His canvases carry titles and are manifestly dedicated to translating bare expression into symbolic statement.

Like Rothko, it has taken Waisler a virtual lifetime to achieve his most seminal work. Where Rothko worked especially with colour washes and dyes to minimise the tactile, Waisler has developed a painting technique to emphasise the palpable nature of his colour fields, which layer by layer achieve great mysterious strength. Waisler's colour system is a reinvention of the spectrum. Precise releases of energy across the canvas have the effect of creating space in depth. It is a radical reconstruction of colour experience and like Rothko's, Waisler's canvases exist in order not so much to dwarf as to silence the spectator and to oust rival visual distraction. But beyond Rothko, Waisler's colours develop a symbol energy which takes the spectator past their surface statements; the colours cease somehow to be the clothing of the natural world, to become voices. Where Rothko's colours converged gradually and inexorably to the black, Waisler's colours emerge from the black.

Waisler has been described as a minimalist. This is erroneous. He may share with the minimalist school an austerity of expression but that is not in order to paint himself out of the perspective but in order to explore again with careful coherence the realms of meaning. Lee Waisler has a point of view, with a magnitude of feeling which springs from the resolution of the assembled thematic tasks which he undertakes to express in symbolic forms.

9

THE LOCATION OF MEANING

For every modern artist of note it has been and remains the unaltered primary dilemma, that he or she must devise and elaborate the language of art in their own idiom before they may hope to reach the point of expression. Both medium and message emerge, as it were, from the same paint pot.

It follows that the finer points of an artist's personal discourse with precedent, and the ways in which his voice happens to join in the colloquy of perceptions which influence his generation, afford only a first sighting to an understanding of his own work. Not only is it the case that the more idiolectic his vision, the greater must be the force and directness of his own contribution; but the face of an artist will always veer in the direction of the unexplored, away from past and current expression. He always stands as the first in his line of vision; we in his reflection. What is fresh in him refreshes us. Hence the primacy of meaning.

Waisler works concurrently in at least four modes. There are the drawings and the sculptures, there are prints and, above all, there are the paintings. Each mode is assigned a continuous role in furthering the overall discourse for meaning in which the artist is engaged. (The roles do overlap, but may be conveniently kept distinct).

10

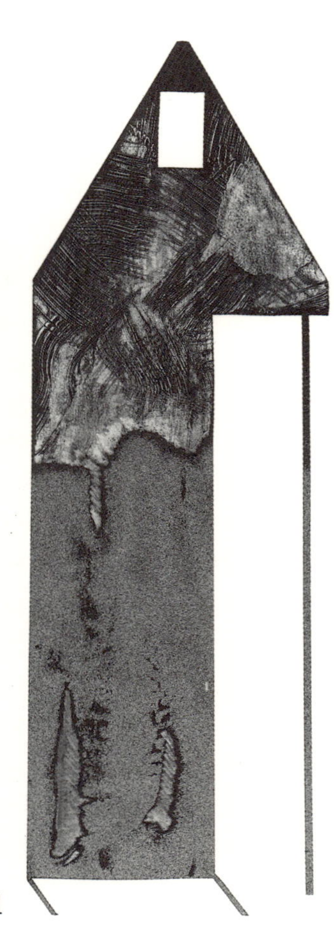

11

12

THE DRAWINGS AND THE SCULPTURES

The contemporary artist, creating as he may, *ex nihilo*, to canons which he develops himself and for himself, will constantly need to explore his own artistic parameters. Waisler's drawings are these explorations and they have the peculiar simplicity and privacy of a conversation with oneself. They are studies in location and dislocation, the search for the stable moments to be derived from the phenomena of instability, the simple lines to give focus to the inchoate. Here the artist confronts the polarities of emptiness on the one hand and of chaos on the other. Where does form begin — significant form? What are the laws of chaos? What is the effect of the mechanical square of a picture frame upon an empty field or of the random line? What is the point of transition from arbitrary play, of line or form, to a palpable significance? Where does aesthetic sensibility enter upon bare perception? Are there wraiths of life in the emergent material?

It is not insignificant that Waisler frequently uses razors direct on carefully receptive paper for drawing. His lines in consequence are always more than lines; they hover at the point of becoming shape, and they have depth. These lineshapes are frequently marked in ground walnut — a colour of particular

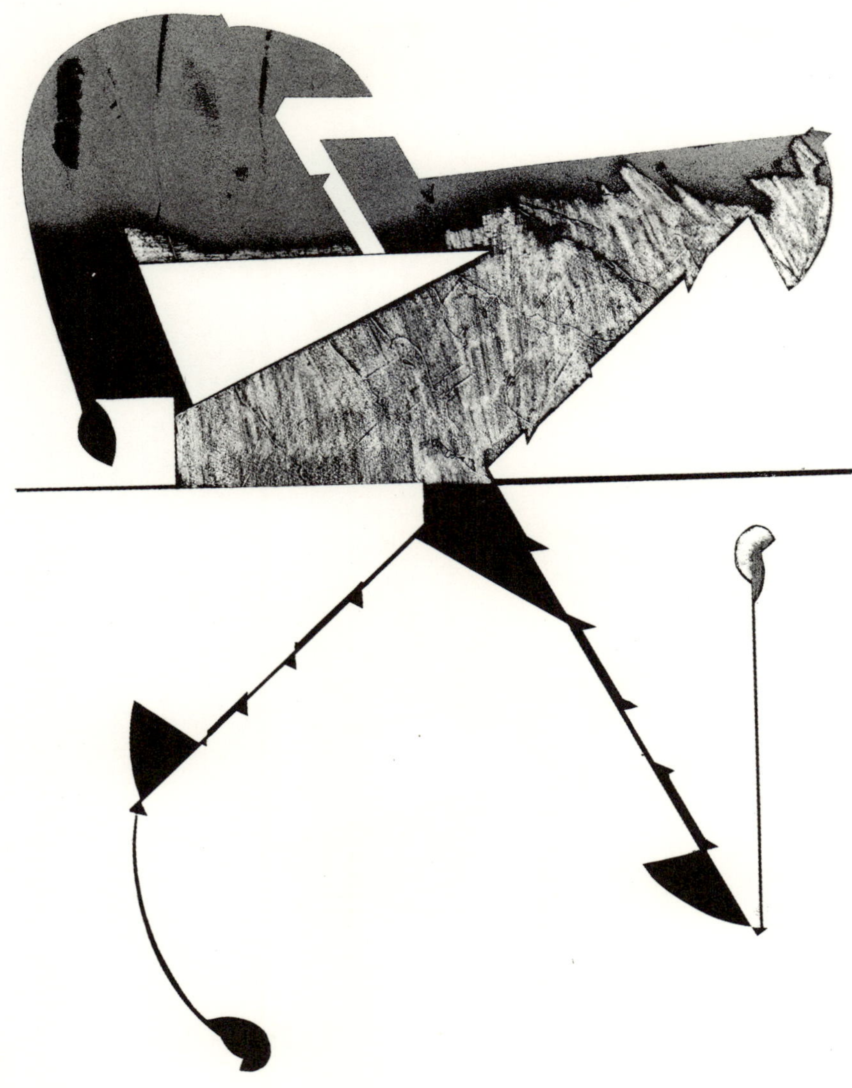

15

warmth and subtlety drawing upon the qualities of a truly living substance, as distinct from a prepared, chemical dye. The entire process is resonant of symbolisms yet to be articulated.

Duchamp, 60 years before, had confronted the phenomenon of an art without rules, devising an aesthetic of random association. That opus was full of the intrigue of the fragmentary — classical learning, erotic fantasy, personal intuition, dream reverie, jokes — order dissolving in chaos, entropy, and then caught in the fleeting eye of aesthetic perception. Paul Klee, with a different temperament and remaining as yet in an ethereally human framework of reference, was in a not dissimilar fashion dismantling the solid in search of the real in art.

One may see the stylistic influence both of Duchamp and of Klee in Waisler's drawings. But the arrow of time is now pointing in the other direction. Where Duchamp and Klee were descending, Waisler is ascending — moving upwards towards the recovery of telling form, and working at the

16

point where meaning and symbolism tremble at the edge of recognition.

It is also the point of commitment (working with razors), where the artist himself must stand with his hand poised, incising the marks of reality upon the face of his paper. The drawings are about the act of creation itself; musings about the working hand and the worked product in a single reflection. The location of meaning is being marked out in delicate, minimalist incisions, to show the moments when and where and how form may resume its dominion.

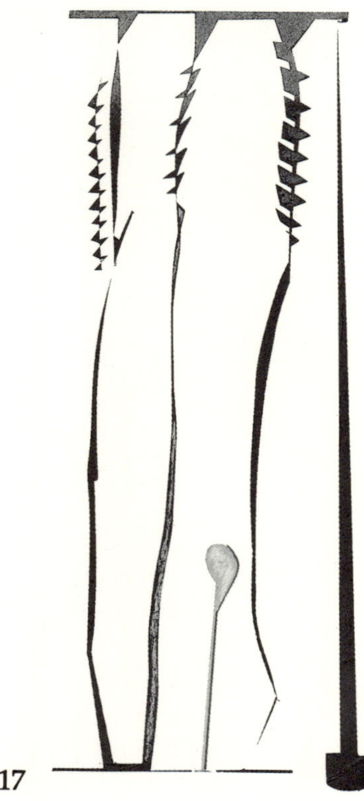

17

It is possibly startling that Waisler would wish to do with sculpture what he does in his drawings; but not only is it of the essence of his instinct for expression that it be large, that is to say of a magnitude greater than the conventional human scale, but also that it must correspond in three-dimensional settings to what the razor might achieve more tentatively on two-dimensional paper: a commitment to significant form. The sculptures, much like the drawings, act somewhat like lenses upon their surroundings in order to give them focus as the proper field of vision. Notably, many of the sculptural essays remain skeletal or linear in form, much as the drawings are apt to be, and they always are oriented towards their adjoining space. Waisler is in fact a sculptor by instinct, a point which repeatedly suggests itself in his drawings and in his canvases; see, for example, the *Stone Oaths*. He works as form-giver and in that he may owe something to Giacometti, whose reticular forms created a repertoire of expression which owed nothing to the meanings of public or private experience previously accepted and everything to the force of its own statements. For Lee Waisler also, meaning is located *in* the forms of his work; its truth in his craft and in his materials and their symbolic power to locate visual meaning.

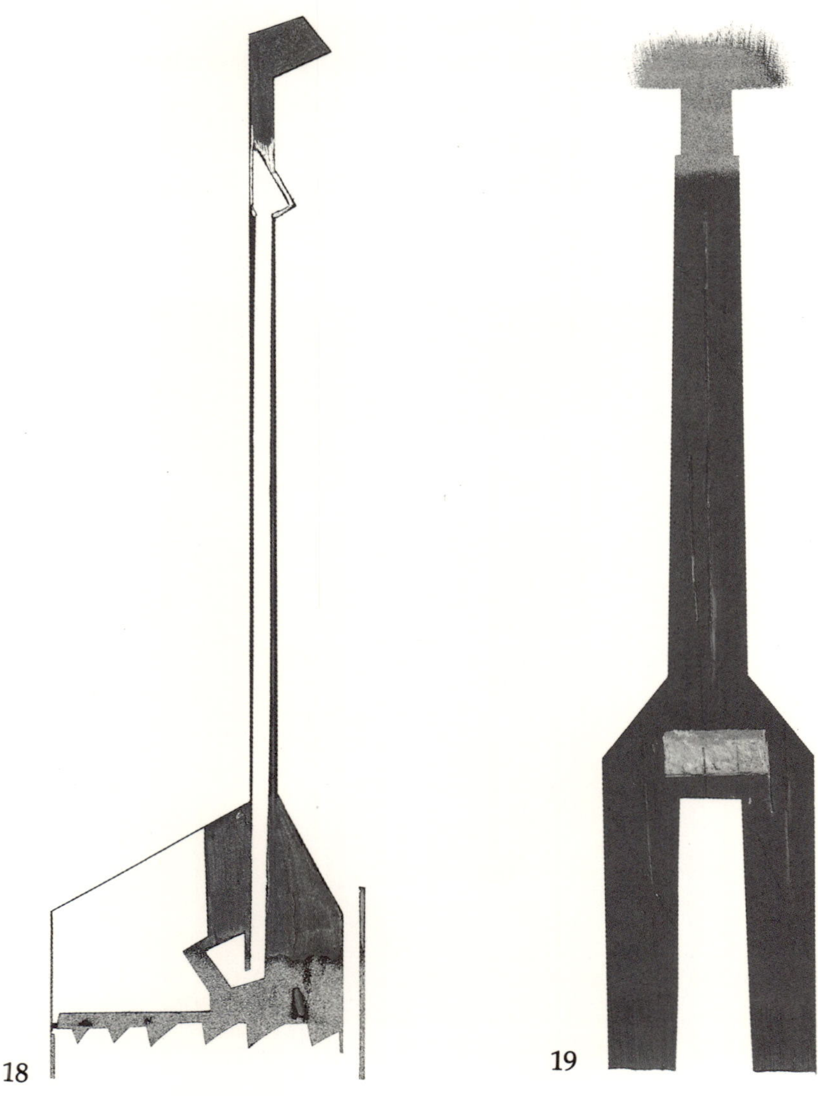

18

19

GRAPHIC WORK

In his drawings and sculpture, one may see the artist striving towards the incipient symbolisation of forms, where meaning has its beginnings. The prints are most often given to his response to memory and tradition and to the life space of people who have impressed him. A beautiful new series is designed to accompany a new Italian translation of ancient Sanskrit legends: see *Drawings 17* and *18*.

His quest remains the same, namely for the expression in visual terms of the universals of meaning. But they are now to be drawn from the emblems of lives and deaths and poetry, transposed into his own internalised landscape. The gravity of Waisler's respect for other human experience creates a special density in his etchings, as though the burden of life were heavy and portentous, never to be discarded, fragmented though it is.

The contrast to the drawings lies in the fact that Waisler accepts in the etchings existent or extant symbols, or their fragments, validated by his subject matter — see for example *Ties of Blood* or *The Most Travelled Road* — whereas the drawings reach out towards the incipience of symbolic form, free of the burden of human pasts.

20   21

THE PAINTINGS

Waisler's work on canvas occupies the great bulk of his output. The canvases are characteristically of a size to dominate their setting, but that is almost incidental to the magnetism of their real presence. If the metaphor of an artist's language has any significance, it is borne out in these paintings. In them meaning finds location. The paintings have names.

The essence derives from the polarity of the two constituent elements common to all the paintings completed by Waisler in recent years. The first of these elements is an abstract sculptural figure; a reference to universals of experience drawn in wood and laminated directly onto the canvas, with the qualities of a personal signature or a hieratic script. Those images are always set in fields of colour — the second element — of a particular vibrance or energy which functions like chorus does to hero's voice in Greek drama. An example of great brilliance is the large canvas *Dialogue*. Occasionally the abstract figure or form surrounds the field — as in *Freud and Jung*. But the two elements are virtually symbiotic; only together do they offer themselves for what they are and for what they mean: for example, the *Gnomon* canvases.

The bent forms are from the hands of a craftsman. They are worked from old, even ancient, common hardwoods — oak, walnut, ash, etc — collected from Dutch ruins or sea edge or forest floor and turned with patience and skill into a choreography of lines which somehow still carry with them the sense for the elemental plasticity of the material. A favourite is a section of a medieval lintel discarded in rebuilding from a barn in Holland, which still shows the rough-hewn marks of its carpenter. Lee Waisler frequently calls it into play as an emblematic head on canvases which involve a theme touching on the human condition, for example in *Mythic Offering*.

These wood forms are thus endowed with the primary symbolism of their material: its natural condition, its age older than its use, its resilience, its battered, weathered persistence, its association with man's first long struggle with nature and a treasured longevity akin to human memory. The forms are then further ascribed a thematic association, in a range from strictly geometric lines and angles that could refer to rationality and order, to curves and shapes which may have human, natural or cosmological connotations. One example: the frequent use of a single bowed line, resolving in its movement of tensed force the contrasting geometric spaces created by straight lines, as in *Triptych First Subject*. The range is extensive and it is recurrent; precisely what might be expected of an articulated, 'hierographic' *language* of art.

The same forms may have more than one significance. It is central to Waisler's approach that he tends to work in series of canvases — for example, the *Stone Oath* group — in which he develops the thematic potential of his forms through variations. A symbol form acts like a question or a problem, and in seeking its answer the artist provokes more questions; the answers remain behind, like experience is left behind, a conditional attempt at reality partially gained; and he tries again. In that important regard the forms are symbolic figures, not signs. Unlike signs, Waisler's forms have no one assigned meaning but like symbols are abstracts of experience that open out or reiterate in themselves, the multi-layered constants of life. Yet further, they are *acts* of form. They are invocative and are shared, as between artist and his viewer; they bond. They are scarcely ever abstractions drawn from a figurative or narrative, conventional world; and even where that is so and they begin life as signs (for example, the painting *Tina* has its inception in a T, taken from a note which Lee Waisler received from his wife) they become statements of being.

Their imagery is not representational but presentational, invoking an inner space and indeed an inner landscape; presence not appearance.

However, in Waisler's paintings form is defined not only by the central symbol but by its field setting, which is never merely background. Though constituted solely of colour and light and without a graphic component, the field setting is itself charged with symbolic force. The symbol forms are, of themselves, always spare and linear and are set, as it were, to searching for their own iconic direction upon this sea of colour and material effect derived from the field setting. It is that setting which gives the forms their energy and impact, their depth of reference or mystery, carrying also the qualities of mood, emotion and human experience (bitterness, tranquillity, abundance, elation, intellectuality) with which any painting of Waisler's will be concerned. A triumphant example of Lee Waisler's searching symbolism is *Triptych*.

Beyond anything that the printed page or photographs can convey, the colour is extraordinary; like layered soil and stone sediment it vibrates in unexpected juxtapositions and blends to convey deep-breathing, slow-moving timebound experience. It is built up physically by dense layers of intensely applied, atomised flecks of separate colourations, some dominant some recessive. Numerous colour layers may be applied and they will hint at all of the mineral wealth of the earth and the life of the sea and the seasons.

Waisler is a symbolist of colour. Some of his paintings consist of several colours of black alone; and black, not white, is the primer of all of his canvases. Black is for him the ground of being, containing not only its darkness but the aura of light to which it aspires. Green appears as the feminine element and in its range and lucidities permeates most of the canvases like an underlying inspiration. Purples and blue signal intellect and the intensities of inward being. Red ranges across the sensations of anger, alarm, anguish but at the same time burns with the forces of life.

Such ascriptions of meaning, colour by colour, are, of course, not to be understood as a set of one-to-one correspondences. Lee Waisler's colours range across each other to explore a universe of felt responses to reality. The language of colour is direct; interpreters do not add anything very much at all.

The earth and its colours are Waisler's palette and they yield for him symbolically the untouchable, ethereal purity and energy of being and the inextricable conjunction of its forces. It remains, however, to communicate or to share that energy with others, those who stand before his canvases and who are to be drawn into them. To this end, Waisler harnesses light; mixing tiny, pin-head beads of glass into his pigments which directionally and selectively reflect light back from the canvas to the viewer. Moreover, as the viewer moves, so does the reflected light; the colours mutate. The whole sculpted painting achieves its dynamic moment at the point when it is seen by eyes which have not painted it!

One speaks of the colour of music in order to describe harmonic qualities in, say, Bruckner or Mahler or Shostakovich. In speaking of Lee Waisler's work one must have recourse to the metaphor in reverse: the music of his colours. His paintings move as music moves through harmonies, dissonances, rhythms, major and minor keys — in fresh, unexpected and idiomatic creations which bond with the bent forms of wood on the canvas, in one statement.

The fascinating result in that bonding is that Waisler achieves a stability and restfulness, even peacefulness, which is to be juxtaposed directly to the temperament of the artist himself, which is tumultuous, and to the themes which preoccupy him, which are mostly disturbing. Lee Waisler working is never far from the raw edge of anguish and anger or the ineluctables of unsettling human emotion, however engendered. The offences of human infamy beat on his artist's awareness like an unsatisfied clamour for sorrow or salvation; echoes of received but discarded meaning jostle in his mind with symbols suffocated in a buried past, praying for reality.

THE RECOVERY OF REALITY

Though he may be, in his paintings, at prayer to no particular god, or wrestling with angels, Waisler's canvases offer the highest possible order of resolution of such conflict. He uncovers meaning, gained from an intense awareness of its loss. The formal is reinstated to signify form, embedded as it is in the spirit of colour drawn from the earth.

One source for the the resultant tranquillity of Waisler's canvases is his craftsmanship. The risks of conscious creation which an artist must take are tempered in his work by a palpable and manifestly accumulated skill and economy of movement and sensitivity in the handling of his materials which carry him directly to the inward moments of his creativity. A safe pair of hands is as much needed by the life-giving artist as by the life-saving surgeon; both stand at the face of creation itself. But it also goes further.

It has been fashionable in the modernist period for artists to place a premium on the notion of the decadence of culture and to link this to an art suggestive of dissolution, dislocation and brutality, which is conveyed not only in subject matter but in the process itself. Fragments of work appear invocative whereas a completed work is impossible; impulses to art may stand as a sufficient statement; disassembled elements are more intriguing than the whole. The self-tortured artist likes to be reflected in his tortured work. It is convenient to reflect upon a terminal condition of art, leaving the unfinished artist to be understood as creating unfinishable work.

In sum, the modernist artist is especially prone to cast himself in the role of a tragic or comic hero of an action drama, in which his own expression forms the subject matter of his depiction. It is less resonant of effect to stay for an outcome when the attempt offers a better pretence at fulfilment. The imperfect is the preferred tense. Contrast this rhetoric or posture with that of a craftsman. Would a craftsman think it to be a valid exercise of his skills to offer to his clients the elements of his product rather than the product itself? No. The craftsman would adhere to that 'classical' assumption, shared unquestioningly in the past by every artist (artists were craftsmen before they 'turned' artist), that he must produce the completed work. The presented product must be the fully resolved solution of the 'problem' with which the craftsman was initially faced. Anything else would be discarded as a workshop failure. However interesting and explicative the gestures of an artist's hand, they are not as such on exhibit until composed into a final, rounded wholeness. However amazing the course of creation, it is its result, at rest from the ardour of its process, which tells the tale: tension set up, sustained, resolved.

22 23 24

In Waisler's paintings one has a conjunction of a craftsman's ethic and an artist's perception. For him, notions of decadence or of crisis in art are, *au fond*, poses which too readily dramatise an artist's loss of faith in any accepted system of human order or reality. They offer a convenient rhetoric of assertion and certainty where no certainty exists. The visual language of most contemporary artists is buoyed by this rhetorical contradiction — as though there were faith to be had in disbelief; but the language itself suffers the defects of its isolation from meaning. That is not Lee Waisler. His visual language is on the way to freeing itself from the rhetorics of artistic isolation and the dilemmas of art based on artistic creativity *in vacuo*. In this his work is on the road to recuperation: dedicated to exploring the scope of visual perception as a vehicle for a signifying inner reality.

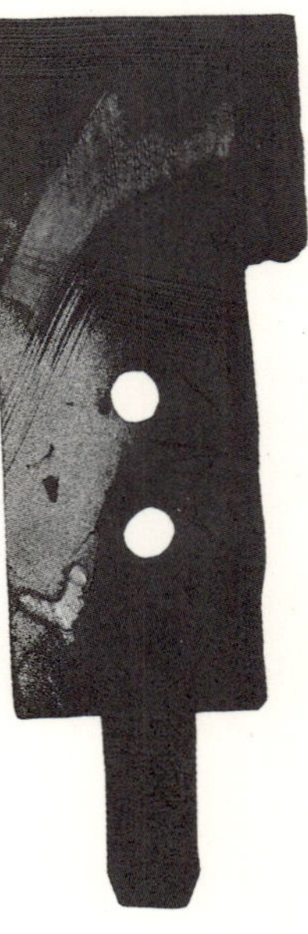

25

Waisler elects to accept a fragmented world to be a long-lived historical fact; not to be associated with a few generations of endangered life but with humanity's nature throughout time. The road to the present is through the deepening (visual) memory of its fragmentary past. See for example the *Three Houses* sculpture, *Fires In The Night* and *Blood Libel*. By a fastidious archaeology of forms Waisler collects on his canvases intact pieces of mnemotic reality, contemporary to him and — perhaps — timeless for the race. It is in many respects a task which might be called an archaeology of the future by virtue of Waisler's total understanding of symbolic function. By twinning simplicity and directness of feeling, expressed in both colour and line, with an enormous respect for the rich time-bound materiality of his media – glass, wood, sand, light, natural pigments — he succeeds in transforming the whole of each of his paintings into a symbol of time itself; that is not arrested time but time distilling from bare materials the worth of a created reality.

Upon that central symbolism, which is recurrent, Waisler then imposes the bent-wood figures (again often recurrent) transecting his canvases like silent, questing symbols of persistent life, charged by dint or glint of his colour fields, with a wondrously fresh vein of simple serenity, for example *Spinoza's Window*. None of these symbols call for elaborate hermeneutics; they may be constructed from the most casual associations, sometimes visual puns, and reduced to the barest of abstractions, but they live in the eye and the memory of the viewer by their 'antiquity'.

Even so, one asks over and again, symbols of what? To this the answer must ever be that it is not to the point to 'translate' symbols; the canvases have names and that, with notes put together for the present book with the help of the artist, must suffice. The heart of the symbolic function is a vision: a bespoken, developing language, one shared or to be shared with the beholder but self-signifying. Valid symbols hold a numinous quality so long as aesthetic means protect the feeling content of the deeper reality to which they refer. In that sense symbols cannot be translated into some other kind of statement; they represent their own meaning.

26

It is an assumption of modern linguistic philosophy that meaning is only conventionally assigned, and that it is impossible to validate meaning by reference to any deeper or metaphysical level outside verbal usages. Truth is tautological as well as fugitive. It is said that one cannot peer behind the veil of language itself. If one could, nothing would be there. That is said to be the central irony of the modern condition, and one may appreciate how modernist art shares that irony in its diverse — and now very tired — pretensions to importance. As George Steiner in his recent book *Real Presences* (Faber,

London 1989; p61) says 'aesthetic perception knows no Archimedean point outside discourse'. There is no referent. Or is there?

There is in the art of Lee Waisler. His language as an artist creates horizons for an inner, symbolic landscape. Indeed it is these horizons upon which his artist's eye is fixed. They expand or change to his perception and it is the presence of these 'frontiers' which, so to say, generate the meaning which is to be discerned in his paintings. It is akin to the colonisation of territory, defined by its boundaries, but designated as 'home' by the exploring pressure upon the horizon: meaning is achieved by its perceived correspondence to truths which lie just beyond the explored limits.

Therein lies the mechanism by which symbols operate. Whereas ordinary humanity is guided by probabilities, the creative artist lives by possibilities. He has no prescribed map to guide him. He develops the symbolic value of his forms as an explorative language which, by its use, locates its meaning to an end just out of sight. He is exploring a perceived unknown; the symbols are his (and our) lodestones. Then, with every new work expressing something of those meanings and some gain upon the undiscovered, however imperfect and partial, pressure builds for yet another attempt. Reality — our reality — is thus not reduced to its limitations but expanded to its (unfathomed) potentials: to the light by which to see and feel and pray.

27

NOTES TO THE ILLUSTRATIONS

Where possible, the observations to the individual illustrations are based on comments of the artist, but they are not otherwise to be understood as being his notes. They are a spectator's observations; and some of the plates are unaccompanied by any comment so as to leave the work to speak for itself.

1 DIALOGUE

An abstract painting, if it is not to result in merest decoration, will contain an element of disturbance or disquiet. In that element the spectator will find the perspective from which to resolve the tensions of the painting.

The source or ground of disquiet in this painting is found in the field of black. Against it are massed forces of colour and line directed to the upper right quadrant. The black is the black of night; not a black which is dead but in which there is light obscured, perhaps to suggest an uncharted darkness against which the dialogue is set, seeking clarity. The striate burnished, grey-bronze gold in the opposing right section, with its suggestion of a fragment from an illuminated manuscript, is the off-setting reference and it generates a sense of freshness which touches the whole painting. There is an allusion not alone to light but to time and to something valued.

It would be correct to understand the painting as a dialogue between both the artist and a spectator, and the artist and his subject. The aesthetic resources of the artist are represented by the gold bronze of the left hemisphere pressing against a resistant *materium*, indicated by the receding, scattered black of the right hemisphere and beyond.

The fact that the linear statement of the painting is geometric, imposed on the canvas in raised fillets of wood, must not disguise the point that it is a drawing; a drawing of a very confident nature which functions like a commitment. Note also how the segmenting green and teak diagonal begins not at the root of the canvas but somewhat higher up, thereby bringing the viewer to the painting at a run and immediately establishing the dynamics inherent in the whole composition.

The meaning and impact of Waisler's colour symbolism can be fully apparent only in front of an actual painting. The cool incandescence and range of his palette is remarkable, as is the texture of the painted canvas and its woven quality. But the most remarkable feature may be the difficulty in actually naming the colours. One is almost led to speak of a re-invention of the spectrum. Yet it is as music is to the ear; the viewer of the paintings is left to supply the essential response which the colour symbolism predicates.

2 SPINOZA'S WINDOW

Waisler has for long been attracted to the Jewish philosopher Baruch Spinoza (1632-1677), a very interesting and most courageous figure. He was in intellectual and moral combat throughout his life but the serenity of his disposition never left him. He earned his living as a lens grinder in the Amsterdam community of Marrano (convert) Jews. He attempted in vain to rejoin his ancestral religion and ended as a recusant to both rabbinical and sacerdotal authority. At a time when the Inquisition was still active and a correspondingly obdurate Judaism insistently imposed *habakha* upon its members, it required a fortified mind to reject revealed truth and to develop a philosophy of immanence in which God and Natural Law were one, depending only upon one's viewpoint. Spinoza was one of the first to set out the case for the ethically autonomous individual, relying on reason and perception alone. He was also one of Europe's earliest proponents of political democracy.

Spinoza's outlook was thus both precarious and embattled. The painting explores this. At the same time it discovers a surprising stability. The lonely perspective of a free thinker and the constraints upon him are symbolised by the narrow opening of the central, tilted configuration. Set against this is a compensating brightness, like filtered sunlight, and the wide arc, shadowed in clear blue suggesting clarity of thought, to give the range and balance of the artist's conception.

3 BLOOD LIBEL

From at least the twelfth century Jews have encountered the totally baseless but ever recurring accusation of the ritual murder of children. The mythic root of this extraordinarily bitter libel, and its offensive link of crime to innocence, appears indefeasible by reason and culture alone. The accusation has been heard even since the Holocaust and its fearful enactment of a crime against millions of innocents — only for being Jews. It lies in the depths of the unconscious.

The thrust of the painting clearly has its starting point in the vital blood-red arc, like an open knife cut, leaping straight across the centre of the canvas up from below its base. The aesthetic of the painting is in its rhythm, which is achieved by the massing of volumes, colour, textures and dimensions against the contrasting statement — one almost wishes to say, voice — of the crimson arch of bent maple. The rhythm in turn sets up a dynamic between the painting and the viewer, who can well spend long hours in front of it, never exhausting its *virtu*.

The sombre black looms over as much as 60% of the surface of the canvas as a deep purple thunder; the eye takes in the burnished shield — or perhaps breastplate — behind a protective wall, and then moves back to the open wound. Can time move wearily along a crescendo of pain? There is no anger; only endurance, the endurance of a people across time. Waisler has found the means of painting time as a human dimension, moving to the centuries of waiting: waiting for the dispensation. *Blood Libel* may be one of the great canvases of the century.

4 PASSAGE   **5** PLOUGHSHARE I

These smaller-sized paintings, in subject matter apparently unconnected with *Blood Libel*, are built up in like manner. However, the symbolic values of the elements are transposed.

In *Passage*, the blue black rectangle represents one of Waisler's central preoccupations — the doorway or passage which obscures that to which it leads. The same theme inspires the major *Stone Oath* series where the doorways are barred and appear false. In other contexts the connotation is to the complexities of an artist's access to his subject. The simple rectangle thus carries the weight of multiple and indeed contradictory significances and is a visual irony to which Waisler is often drawn.

Ploughshare II has great resemblance in form to *Blood Libel*, but it offers an entirely opposing theme: weapon beaten into ploughshare. The bloody wound is now an earthy furrow, the looming black is replaced by a fertile green; the watchful, burdened sense of time and of endurance gives way to a different endurance and to a suggestion of another time, the rhythm of a cyclical living with the implements of an arable existence.

9 STONE OATH ARC   **10** STONE OATH ALARM
11 STONE OATH DANGER   **12** STONE OATH CHIMNEY
13 STONE OATH BURNING   **14** STONE OATH ALTAR

The *Stone Oath* series of paintings is an important, indeed pivotal, part of Waisler's mature *oeuvre*. Simple, geometric forms are mutated symbolically to address or record the artist's preoccupation with the collective memory of a terrible offence.

Both Primo Levi and Paul Celan thought of stone as the emblem of the aftermath to the Holocaust, and so does Waisler. And what is an oath? One may suggest that it is a call before God that a promise shall be kept or, perhaps, that an event shall be remembered. So what is the Stone Oath? A kind of obelisk, a frozen atonement or the symbol of a destiny which is vital to the conscience of the living as much as a tombstone for the dead?

The panels exceed human height and are some 14cm or more deep; thus they function as quasi-sculptures, imposing a symbolic monumentality upon Waisler's statements. Similarly, the colours range widely across his symbolic spectrum, not only depicting the event (or reflecting the artist's own emotion) but transfiguring it to a status bound up with time or history itself.

In the central void of each of the panels the image of the door or passage recurs, already noted in the preceding plates to be of great symbolic weight.

28   29   30

Entrances are not only the access to the passages but afford an intimation of what lies ahead. Waisler's work is full of the transposition of symbols, with a consequent inflection in their meaning. Here the emphatic vertical column barring these entrances is directly derived from the identical imagery from which the *Bookburners,* another series, take theirs: the furnaces of the death camps, standing like some damned obsequy in the way of the living. Waisler comments: 'I make my paintings to be things and not pictures of things.' The symbols are at the threshold of reality. They *are* the entrances.

Waisler recalls how in his childhood he had the household chore of burning waste every day in the backyard of his home in an incinerator very similar to those he has painted. He also recalls that the news of Auschwitz first trickled through to the West in those years. Since then, those incinerators have remained with him as an unfulfilled consummation, as though it was for him to have been consumed in them. Thus an end always has its beginnings, full of dread, an unlived life and an undying death.

The contrast between *Stone Oath Chimney* and *Stone Oath Burning* stems from the artist's emotional response to his subject. The second is evidently nearer to a visualisation of the very act of burning in a consuming heat, whereas the first is further removed from the event. Only the apex in ashen grey signals the connection, but the furnace is cold. So is there perhaps a passage past the barred doorway? Was the bar to guard against the furnace or is the whole thing a false prospect? It is a burning question for the spectator, if there can be a spectator.

The somewhat smaller paintings of *Stone Oath Alarm* and *Stone Oath Danger* offer a slightly modified 'message'. The theme of the false passage is lifted high, almost like a road sign to signify either warning or direction. The colours of *Alarm* are warm bronze, brown to sea green and peach rust and they are quieter than the much more alarming message of *Danger*, with its red oxides and blue black ash colours. *Burning* speaks ineluctably of a kiln or furnace door. The association is unmistakable and the theme of the false passage turns obviously ominous.

While *Alarm* and *Danger* are presented as signs, though they may also be objects, *Stone Oath Arc* is the pure objective symbol. Its colours suggest the working of time upon its form. Its monumental character is reinforced by the arc which here, contrary to the tension of the arc in *Blood Libel,* is employed as a resolution; a resolution to the question, *is* the passage false? And if it is false, what is then the oath? An oath of denial? The question itself is seemingly cast in stone, and the answer is there to seek — in the symbol.

The climax is reached in *Stone Oath Altar,* the largest and the ultimate of the series. Though the form remains, the dimensions are altered so that the altar's significance appears to be a different one. What was before an object of compulsion has turned into something more universal. Similarly, though the colours continue to subsume the symbolic history conveyed by the earlier panels, they now carry a hint of vitality and of synthesis which suggests that the symbolism itself is moving on, beyond the age of anguish. The vertical and the horizontal axes now cross in balance and the passage has widened. Indeed there may now be two passages. The stone has become more nearly an invitation to pass than the cruel trap it represented at the beginning.

18 RAISED HOUSE, SCULPTURE **19 HOUSE OF JANUS, SCULPTURE**
20 GROUP OF HOUSES, SCULPTURE

Some half metre in height, these sculptures introduce us to a different sphere in Waisler's imagination, as it were the residential section. Waisler has maintained a studio in Holland for many years and has steeped himself affectionately in the history of the close-knit town where it is located. The shape of the house roofs is taken directly from the vernacular architecture of Northeast Holland. But symbolism is not far to seek. These houses might not have been out of place, one thinks, in the early cities of the Chaldeans, nor is it difficult to discern the sense of self-respect and community order in the freely assembled grouping to which these sculptures lend themselves. Nor is Waisler's symbolic vocabulary in a different language from that of the canvases discussed so far, though the idiom may be more popular. As one contemplates the *House of Janus* it comes to mind not only that the ancient god was imbued with the knowledge of both the past and the future but that he was the protector of the doorways.

And to be sure that we draw no assurance or false sense of stability from these groups, Waisler has recourse again to the transposition of symbolic form. House can turn to Furnace.

22 THREE HOUSES

This sculpture in oak of a townscape again speaks of more than itself. The contrast of precise modelling and inexact fenestration and entrances creates a special oscillation in our perception. The houses are also their occupants and carry the signs of their humaity: arms, legs and careful, anxious eyes, and beyond these a hint of watchful welcome.

23 FIRES IN THE NIGHT

In this painting Waisler explores what it might have meant for children to see the concentration camps. How might they have understood what they beheld? He paints their fantasy: incomprehensible fires of extinction upon the glowing images of home. The anguish of that period filtered by troubled innocence creates an extraordinary visual poetry and leaves an undying lament intact for other generations.

24 SHELTER I   **25** SHELTER II

Mankind has not always needed homes, only shelter. The trace of the prairie dwellers and of the desert nomads is now largely in our dreams, in archetypal figures. But it remains for the artist to ensure that these ancestral ghosts are not neglected.

26 TABERNACLE

Before the Jews ever achieved any permanence of place, they strove to provide a sanctuary, perhaps only a tent, for their indwelling God. For Waisler the symbols of indwelling coalesce with the sense of the whole and integrated individual, at one with the forces of the unconscious. Thus this painting is about two houses and about the space beyond the painting itself from which its nourishment is drawn; the home respectively of the spiritual and, beneath it, of the non-spiritual.

As with so many of Waisler's paintings, the colour field is the dominant source of influence upon the viewer; the yellow regenerative light tells that sanctuary is within. Nor is it without significance that the precise colour values can scarcely be named. The effect is all: the symbol of a sensibility.

27 FREUD AND JUNG

Waisler's symbolism is always transformational. The forms of shelter reappear in the gothic shape of two facing figures, representing the two great master mariners of the unconscious. As is well known, Freud and Jung's personal and professional relationship ended in anger and left both men and their followers morally scarred. But the drama of that conflict remains a paradigm of the modern soul's unrequited and indeed divided search for — shelter. Are the two explorers joined, like the hemispheres of the brain, across a central insight or competing for it? Either way, the symbolisation is very compelling, quoting, as it appears to do, also from Matisse's *Vestments of St Dominic* and in the perhaps unintentional outline of hands in prayer.

28 PROTO-TINA

A study in a more personal vein and the first in a series concerning the artist's wife, herself a figurative artist. It is a painting of discovery. The stick figure motif is a reference to the ancient convention of a hunter's magic markings, to capture the fugitive creature of nature. The small solid red copper rectangle at the left side of the painting is a simple metaphor for stolid middle age in contrast to which the tripodal figure is gaily elusive. The gestural drawing is balanced by blue mauve in the colour field, with its hint of seriousness of feeling.

29 TINA I

The male/female encounter is quite explicit, the outline form of the pervasively feminine contrasted by *indicia* of male conquest, rational and sexual. The painting may owe a debt to Duchamp but it leaves no question that the feminine element will triumph. It is the colour field which creates the aesthetic balance for the abstract figure.

On the subject of abstraction, the artist tells the story of Mr Zeretski. Mr Zeretski was a tailor and a family acquaintance from the old country, who worked with paper dress patterns, marking out his cloth with the waxy sliver of grey tailor's chalk used in his trade. 'I saw him work as a child. To me the yellow paper patterns and the chalk lines were pure abstractions, and like Mr Zeretski I consider that I generate reality from the abstract rather than the other way about.'

30 TINA II

Waisler painted this canvas at the climax of courtship and he takes the characteristic T of his wife's signature as the graphic parable of her impact upon him. Everything that matters to the artist appears to be brought under the umbrella of her presence. One notes Waisler's care to draw a thin line of black, like a nerve, along the surface of the vertical oak as though to belie the bare abstraction, but the full sense of feeling which the painting is intent upon conveying is to be found in the colour scheme. The more usual, pre-eminent black has been largely suppressed. Colours of blue and gold are suffused with brightness, conveying the artist's exuberant mood and a lightness of being not so far seen in his work.

31 FUNNEL

Waisler's work is notably free of self-reference. There is however a group of paintings which is dedicated to the symbols of the artistic process. The first is concerned with the image of the red-hot furnace. It requires little comment save to emphasise how imposing it appears in its own space in full dimension and to note that it contains the outlines of the same form as is found in the *Bookburner* series. It reflects Waisler's sense for the ambivalence of symbols and, beyond them, for the ironies which they may represent.

32 ALCHEMY I

If it be accepted that the artist has the gift of creation, that is to transform what is base or ordinary into something perceived to have value — and indeed to transform our perception of nature itself — then ancient alchemy is his perfect symbol.

No alchemist has ever made gold, and Waisler paradigmatically discerns similar limitations in the artist's work. The process of his work is inherently incomplete and, as he says, 'the images that have been revealed obscure their meaning.' Thus the aesthetic dimension is not transformative enough; which also corresponds with the teachings of the alchemists, who insisted that if a man would change nature (base metal into gold) he must first be prepared to change himself. It is also a saying of the Talmud. Yet the artist persists.

He is in Waisler's imagery the maker of passages. In this painting the artist's enterprise is depicted in plan. All the elements — the crucible, the door, the vertical line of the passage deflected into the horizontal — are seen to be disconnected and tentative. This is the record of what, at best, has been an attempt at creation.

33 CRUCIBLE

Waisler next turns to the 'risk' in the artist's ambition to create. The life of an artist is in crucible, and in the creative act there is a moment at the very point of ultimate achievement when entropy intrudes to end the artist's work and even his life.

The painting refers to the suicide of Mark Rothko. The small square panel is an allusion to his work. The passage traverses the panel, splits it in twain. The elements of the painting are strong but they run inconclusively. The crucible goes cold.

34 ALCHEMY LINTEL

The maker of passages creates an entrance for a passage. A heavy old Dutch wood beam section is put in place by way of lintel. Its horizontal, earth-boundedness is painted over with gold, as if to transmute its nature so that it may have lightness. That fails: the vertical dimension is lacking and the entrance appears to lead to a cave. The bronze is flecked in green; age has overtaken the enterprise, as failure overtakes the artist.

35 ALCHEMIC LAKE

There is an elusive, ancient Egyptian alchemical myth that the sun must cross an underground lake; it is here symbolised by the fluid line, its surface a mirror. The lake is outside the palette of the painter and (observe the right upper segment directly lit) all that he may do is see his own reflection. One is looking at the conceptual format for a mystical landscape where only the imagination may be at home.

36 DIVINING ROD

The subject of the painting, the search for life-giving water, links it to the *Alchemic Lake*, but the quest is now more 'earthy'. Water is itself a symbol for the spirit and the colour symbolism, suggesting an ancient and deep-lying soil, is the ground over which the questing probe is reaching. What does the earth hold and how may it be 'divine-d'? And to the left of the probe is there a glimpse of lode?

37 CALLING TOWER

The task an artist undertakes in 'making' symbols is charged with questions. Symbols are the product of time, resting on long established convention and accruing qualities. What then is the process of transformation which turns bare elements of colour and line into an object which is an invocation of meaning?

The woods on this canvas are oak and maranta, the latter from the disappearing rain forests and on the edge of extinction. Waisler places it at the apex of the painting to emphasise its rarity and to point a paradox: is it possible to create something of value without a corresponding act of use or destruction?

The black of the painting is in fact built up in several layers of brown-near-to-black and this creates an ambient field for the slender lines of the upward sweep of the structure which is warm, with a suggestion of the ethereal. The only true black is inside the frame and this is much colder in contrast.

The eye or lens theme of the maranta is one which Waisler has used in other paintings to suggest inspiration or clarity of vision. Here it is consistent with the idea of a silent or mystical call which punctuates a very graceful and still composition.

Another painting about the 'making' of symbols is *Mythic Offering*. It is also largely in black — a black which is here a living colour, akin to alluvial soil rich in its fertility and full of movement, symbolising life's processes that silently, timelessly, unconsciously configure its course. The artist achieves the effect of vitality by mixing green with the black. The rectangle is at the point where it becomes an 'altar', but only just. It is an altar to no one. However, the 'offering' is once more a wood section taken from the salvaged medieval building beam which so frequently figures in Waisler's current repertoire of forms as an emblem of human care and work and of time.

38 METRONOME

Like an essay in contemplation, the painting juxtaposes a symbol of historical time to the segmentation of a metronome, and leaves the viewer to share with the artist the questions which arise.

39 **TRANSPOSITIONS**

Waisler's abstract forms explore meaning by transposition and colour. Convenient visual assumptions are quietly unsettled, perspective is not fixed and balance is left just short of stability. Forms which appear to suggest funnels in one painting speak of passageways in another. Colour moves dynamically. Positive can flick over into negative. All this is carefully judged by the artist, in order to alert the viewer into the transformative act of painting itself: to be not an onlooker but a respondent, as though at the point of joining a discussion, to supply the 'moment' of resolution which the painting seeks.

40 **GNOMON ALTAR I**

In the Gnomon series of paintings, spanning nearly a decade, Waisler has created the core of his experiments in abstract symbolism. This early example, with its luminous central blue panel offset by clean black, has great delicacy within its strict, formal framework and might not be out of place in a Persian illuminated manuscript.

The title Gnomon Altar itself carries considerable charge. The word gnomon is related both to the Greek gnosis (knowledge) and gnomon (sign) as well as to Paracelsus' guardian of the earth's treasures. James Joyce used the word as a pun 'to know man'. It also is the name for the device on sundials by the shadow of which for centuries we have told time. Plato's myth of the cave comes to mind: all we know is by shadows and reality lies beyond.

41 **GNOMON ALTAR II**

The artist is working on the idea that an altar, and all that it might stand for, should not be at rest. The left arc sweeps upward beyond the formal rectangle and acts to unbalance it, as though to introduce a dynamic into an otherwise too rigid (doctrinal) formalism. The search must continue — for another (alter)!

42 **GNOMON OFFERING**

The rich colours of burned sienna and rose are a far cry from the still, contemplative panel of the *Gnomon Altars*, and they suggest a more subjective, troubled presence. Is this no man's altar, the altar of the forsaken, or is it the altar that has been forsaken?

43, 44, 45 **TRIPTYCH FIRST SUBJECT, SECOND SUBJECT, THIRD SUBJECT**

Symbols can never be made. They must either be found or they must evolve. Therein lies one of the constraints of Waisler's exploration of symbols.

The origin of these three magnificent panels was in a painting, *Ascent — Descent* in which the artist was working on the dilemma of the 'made' symbol, as he had in *Calling Tower* and *Mythic Offering*. A simple configuration of ascendant, descendant steps, constructed on canvas with pieces of maple and oak in a very approximate symmetry, were linked to a light-reflective line of vertical black. The result was a geometric pattern suggesting an ancient, possibly American Indian sacred motif. But the painting lacked statement and was perhaps too nearly decorative. Waisler destroyed it. What he was searching for lay too far beyond the visibilities on that canvas.

However, he was immediately led to a new sequence of panels, in which the ascent-descent motif was transformed into something of much greater weight and subject matter. In three canvases, forming a triptych, one is instantly taken to the outlines of an early (though unidentified) religious architecture.

Each panel is now endowed with the shape of the ascendant-descendant steps, first reaching up to a well-defined platform and then returning in rough symmetry back down to the main body of the painting. The resulting simplicity of form is balanced by colours of great emotional directness and luminous intensity. It is very tempting to associate this balance with a reference on the one hand to an authoritative and hieratic community and on the other hand to deep personal devotion. The symbolism remains, however, quite innominate, as no doubt the artist intends it to be. Yet that only reinforces the impact of the triptych. The theocentricity is implicit. There is much in these three paintings which is akin to the famous Rothko chapel in Houston, Texas.

First Subject was created first and has all the appearance of the greater youth. The sprung sweep of the oak wood overrides the plane of the picture, reaching up from the very base of the painting beyond its peak, and has about it an inspired impatience as though to short-cut the steps and to speed personal aspiration. The colours too are in consonance and are made to swirl up, reaching from a contoured ground that appears freshly excavated.

The form of the *Second Subject* panel is significantly modulated. The *First*'s striving is now a focused restatement in the emblem of a wooden window or eye, the epitome of the original aspiration. The fiery red colour drapes the edifice in a both rich and ascetic tapestry, as though to convey yet greater strength of feeling. The right of the canvas has been palette-knived to accentuate the time-worn appearance of the panel, echoing in turn the actual age of the central beam section at the top of the panel. A vision has been validated.

Having apparently achieved in *Second Subject* a synthesis of spiritual intuition, Waisler embarks in *Third Subject* upon a radical departure. All worldly or historical associations descend into the timeless black ground of being. One notes both the dramatic loss of colour and the gouged lines into the black: black under black. The device is duplex. On the one hand, the lines hint at the depths in the black, as though to admit light, and on the other hand the lines are intentionally incoherent and lack the artist's usual linearity and

31

tension. Is not the blackness womb to a rebirth and are these not the striations of the newborn? From the apex, gold flows as though it were a dispensation. An abstract vision has turned into a source of light. The wood section is turned about and takes on the form of a Hebraic letter: the letter for life, chi.

46 THE MESSIAH MYTH

As the artist carves out from a transcendent silence the felt meaning of his existence, the question is does the silence bear a relation to the meaning? Is there a dialogue?

One should let the eye first dwell on the colours of this painting, moving from the obscurity of the left lower corner past the extraordinary cloud of blue, grey and green over a foundation of oxidised red, to the right sector of bronze light gradually darkening back in a red tinge of desert shadow. Then consider the choric effect so achieved against the simple wooden drawing of the incomplete passage on one side of a long, finely-tapered vertical in teak, and that vertical then held down by the thorns of rejection set into the impassable horizontal. One is left with just the one question, and it is the painting which asks it: what has happened to the Deliverer of the Jews?

Then, past the desolation of the Shoah and on the far side of the irredeemable, something stirs. Those who must breathe in the after day of death find that the pulse of life presses through the cinders of defilement to waken the senses afresh. What cannot be collectively borne is individually reborn – upon the one cross. In the remaining sequence of paintings – all completed immediately after *The Messiah Myth* – Waisler is to be seen at work upon individuation.

47 PHOENIX

The bold figure, half-winged creature half crucified man in *Phoenix*, is in remarkable juxtaposition to the preceding *Messiah Myth*, in which the elements are so barely assembled and so fragile. A different voice is being heard from: the voice of survival.

48 DIASPORA

Diaspora has the same positive vigour. Still upon the cross, the elements of man are not just hung but flung back into the field of the living – a dispersal which is more like the spread of seed than the fragmentation of a race.

49 TIMEKEEPER I

The painting of course refers directly to the subject of the earlier *Triptych* (Plates 43-45), but now boldly centres upon a mandala, the symbol of individuation. The canvas is also one of a triptych, in each of which a golden, segmented circle is set in colour fields of varying intensity fusing black, rust, sand and gold. Each circle is incomplete but reads as a sundial, encoding the day, the month and the year of the artist's birth. Time keeps the keeper and the keeper keeps time. He is the sun; he is the son.

Far from being egocentric in effect, the painting is wholly objective. The underlying subjective disturbance, elsewhere so manifest in Waisler's work, appears resolved into a mode of imbued awareness, a statement of the luminous self, a self which can speak for itself unaided. The mandala and the shape of the canvas together become more plainly one fused symbol of man's presence: head, shoulders and a body endowed with a soul, saying to us: 'I do not know what you would want that you do not already have.'

50 CRUCIBLE II

For Waisler it is life which is the crucible and death its extinction. Life is pain, death is peace and each belongs to the one receding crown of vision:

> The deepest offence
> now drifts upon the after day
> like a pall ascending
> from an altar of their ash
> – the graven, long dying –
> in the clear light
> of a perfect dream,
> their death my hearth,
> a vision crowning
> each their end.

Both this painting and the next have as an integral element surrounds of zebra wood, purple heart wood and padauk wood, all of which are endangered species – along with man.

51 PAX

Pax was occasioned by the terminal illness of a very gallant acquaintance, and memorialises the spirit of someone who chose death than let it choose him. It is an exit painting. One notes the very black 'entrance' receding behind the canvas. It is as though a man were departing into a landscape (it might have been painted by Turner) composed of ash and light, and one remembers that black in the colour vocabulary of Waisler is the ground of being.

POINT OF DEPARTURE
BY LEE WAISLER

The Hollywood of my early childhood still shone in a pre-polluted light, strangely defiant of the war news that filtered into our awareness. The war raged on until I was seven; over there, of course.

When I was thirteen, my family moved north of the city, to a lifeless hamlet bound and gagged by the wash 'n wear fabric that was the American 50s. It was then, sitting alone at a huge linoleum-topped table in my school library, that I studied the photographic documentation of the German death factories. I stared at the massed mounds of dead. I searched their faces. They disintegrated into patterns while the surrounding posts, windows and stones remained intact, symbolic monuments to the lost lives. Incredulous and inadequate, unable to absorb the implication of those shocking images, I imagined myself to be among the victims: captive, escaping, conspiring, even collaborating in order to survive.

Only years later did I realise why my identification with the victims was incomplete. I was not there, and it laid a ground of guilt that would shape my perceptions and direct my conduct. Reluctantly, I had to accept the dilemma of the observer, my sense of isolation reinforced by the narrow perspectives of an illiberal community. The Holocaust necessarily became the tableau against which I projected my own life. Yet I was constrained from painting it, as though there was profanity in any attempt to transform the catastrophe into an aesthetic.

By another yardstick, the task appeared to be the reconciliation of the future to its past. I would ask you to imagine standing at the centre of a narrow foot-bridge. One end of the bridge denotes the past while the other denotes the future. Neither end is discernible and you are unclear as to which is which. Yet you are extraordinarily alert: you sense certain shapes and colours and time moving at an unfamiliar pace. You try to place these things into a logical relationship, but you cannot. You realise that logic is insufficient as a means of making sense of this experience — this place. You look inwards, as though dreaming. You notice at your feet the raw materials of the artist. You instantly and intuitively understand some of the ways in which you can use these materials and quite naturally you begin painting. Your need is to give form to your experience of standing at the centre of the footbridge. Yet you know that as the images reveal themselves their meaning recedes. They will not release their mystery. But, to your surprise, in those shadows a form appears. Could it be yourself?

Through Freud I had seen the self defined as paramount. Had not the Nazis (and others) subordinated the self to the *Volk* or the masses or the media, and thrust the world into despair? Driven by a sense of responsibility to sustain the individual, I began to work.

1

2

3

4

5

6

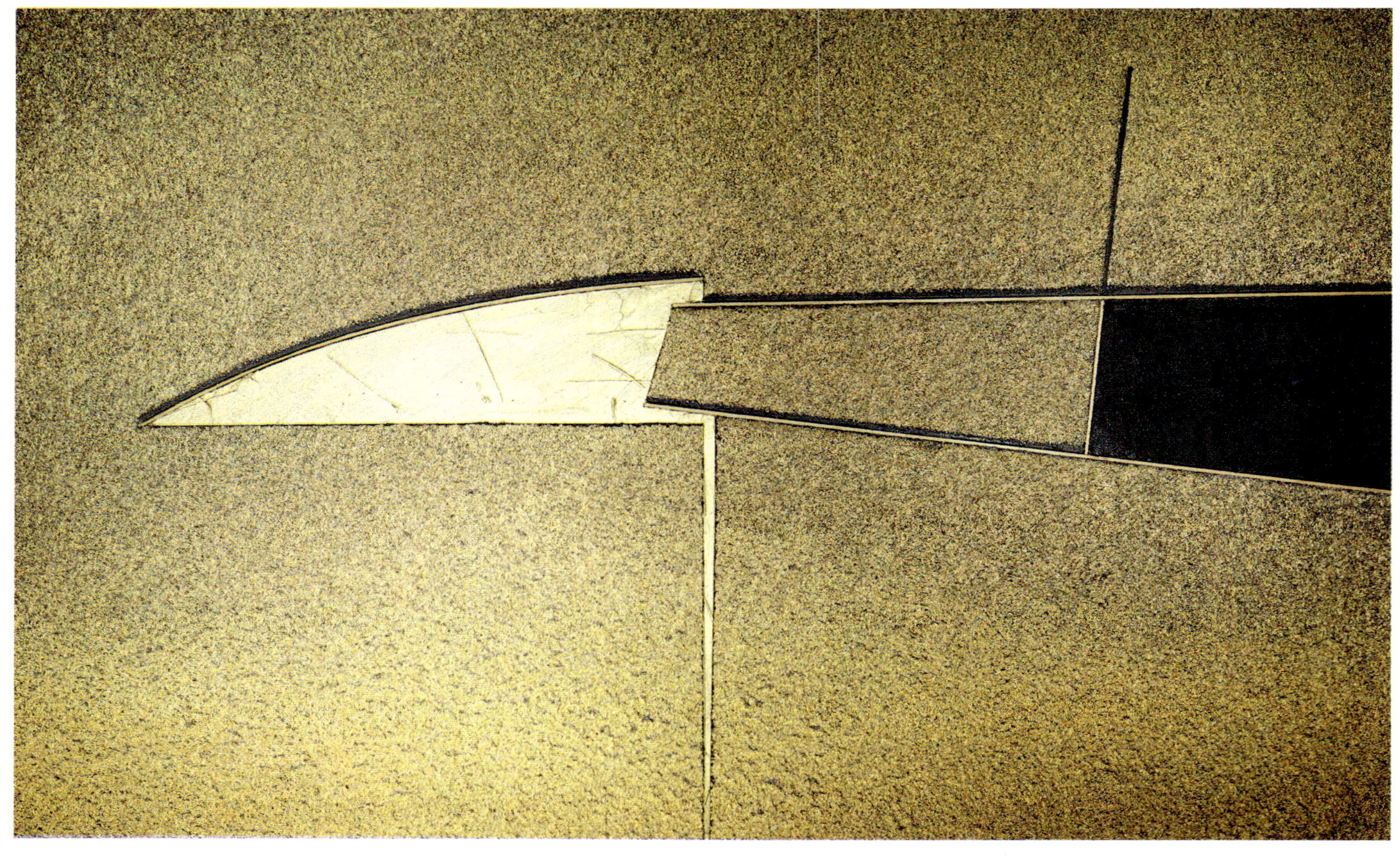

7

13

15

17

18

19

21

22

23

24

25

27

31

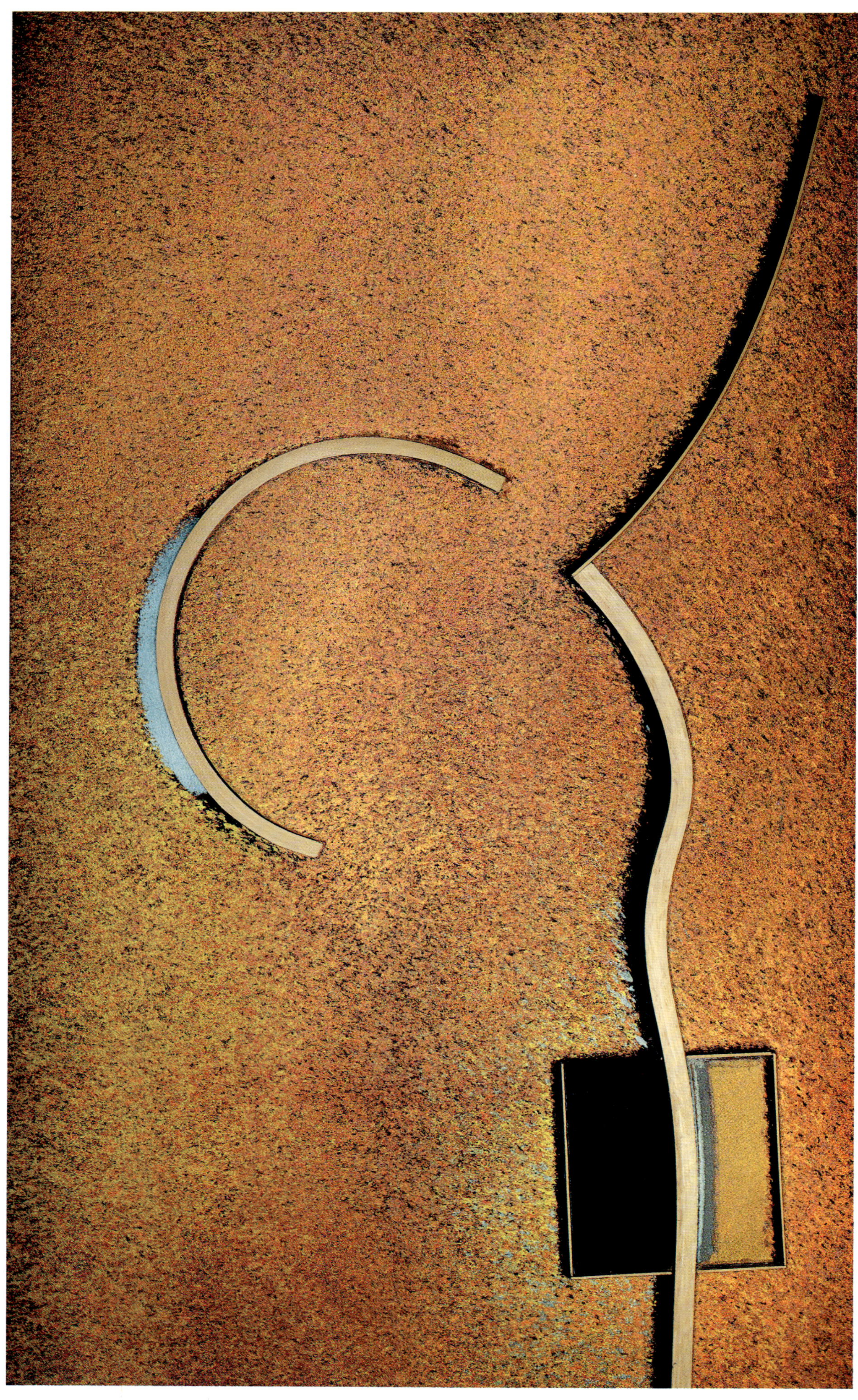

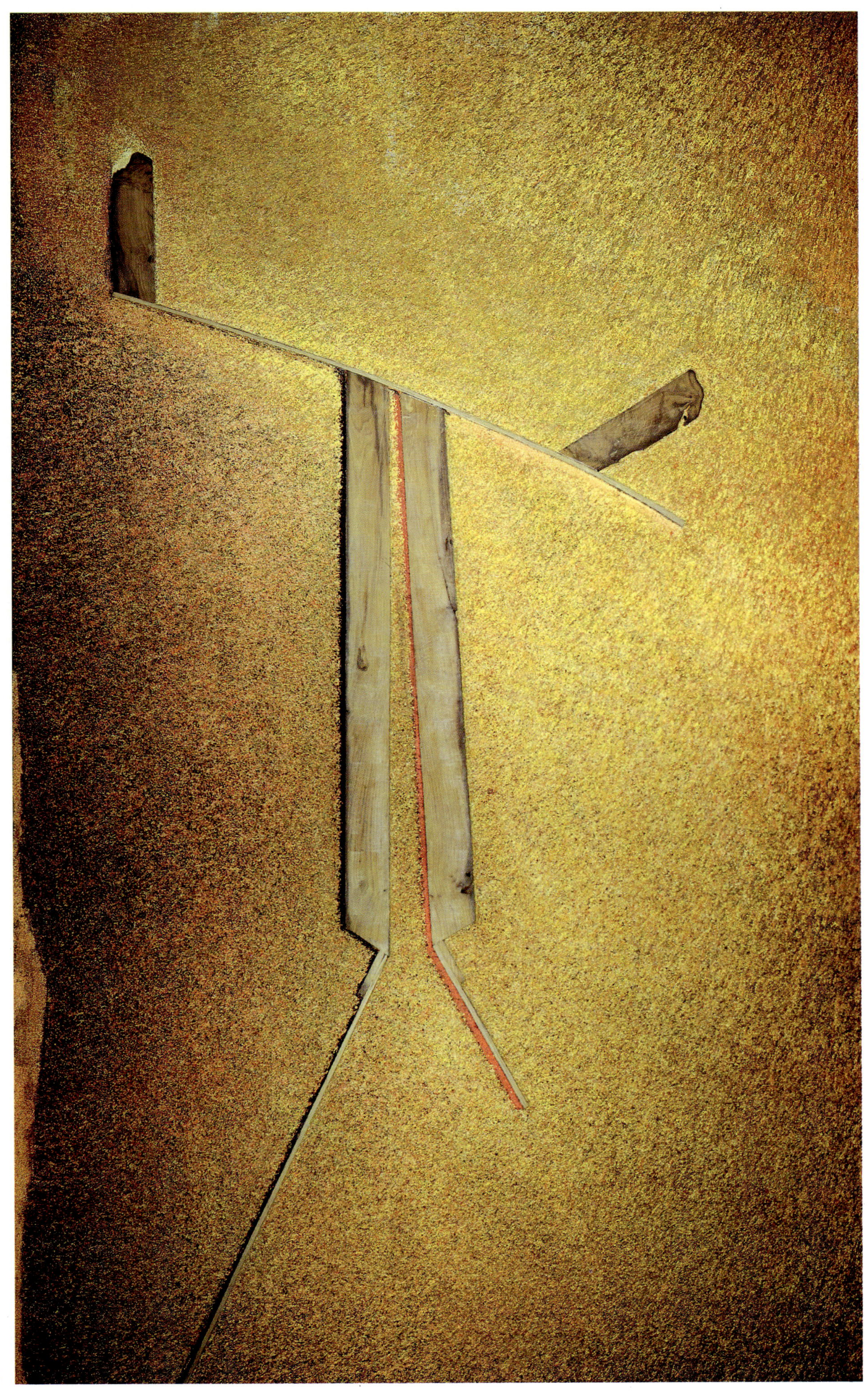

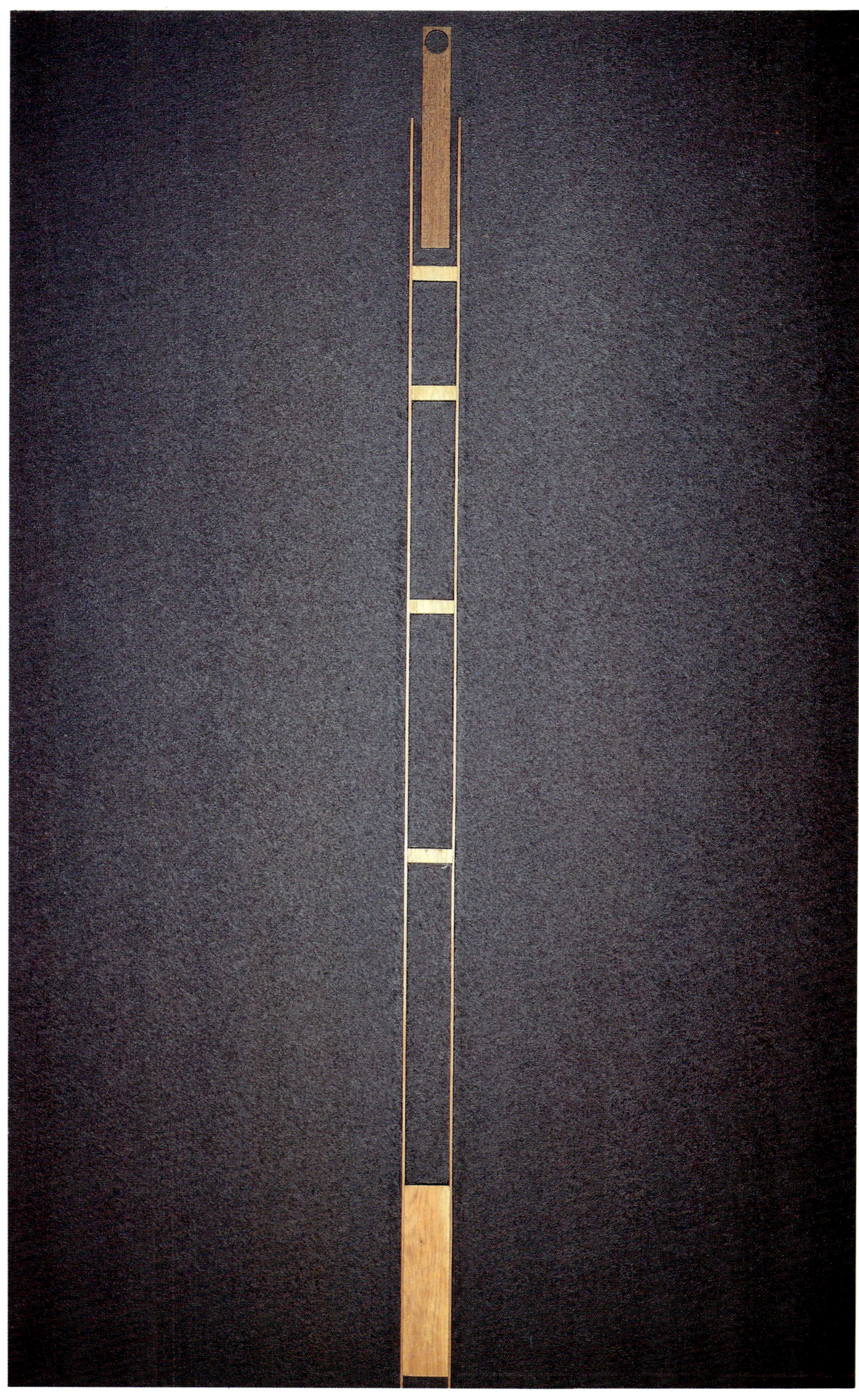

41

43

44

45

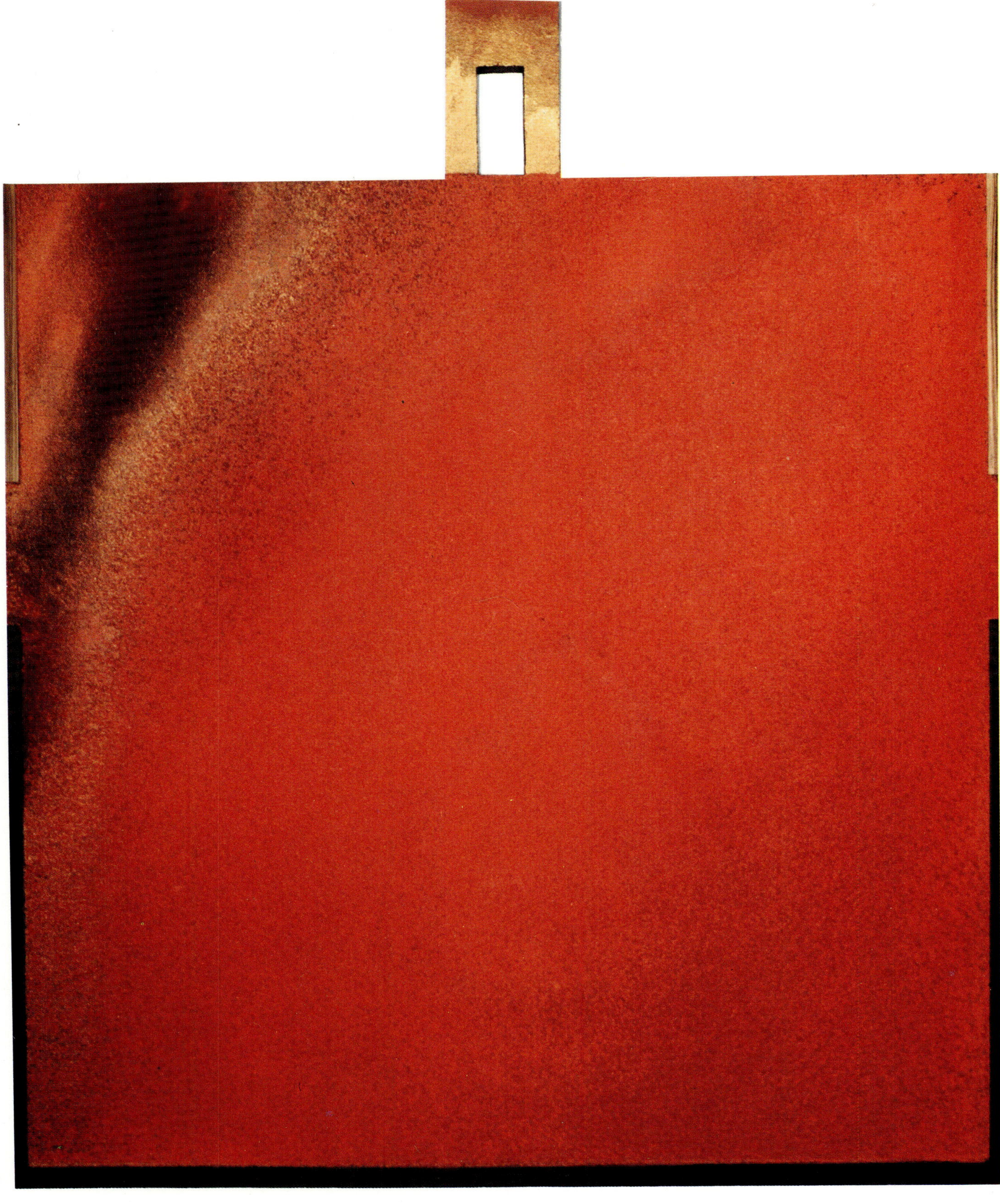

51

LIST OF ILLUSTRATIONS

Unless otherwise stated, all measurements are in centimetres.

ILLUSTRATIONS IN THE TEXT

1   Unnamed drawing
Acrylic and graphite on paper
76 × 56

2   Unnamed drawing
Acrylic, graphite and walnut shell on paper
76 × 56

3   Days of Vigil (Primo Levi Suite)   1986
Relief etching on paper
99 × 69

4   The Night Held Ugly Surprises (Primo Levi Suite)   1986
Relief etching on paper
99 × 69

5   A Hard Voice (Primo Levi Suite)   1986
Relief etching on paper
99 × 69

6, 7, 8 Under the Mushroom   1985
Inflatable sculpture in black ripstop nylon
15 × 15 × 15m

9   Unnamed drawing
Acrylic on paper
76 × 56

10   Unnamed drawing
Acrylic and graphite on paper
76 × 56

11   Unnamed drawing
Acrylic, graphite and walnut shell on paper
76 × 56

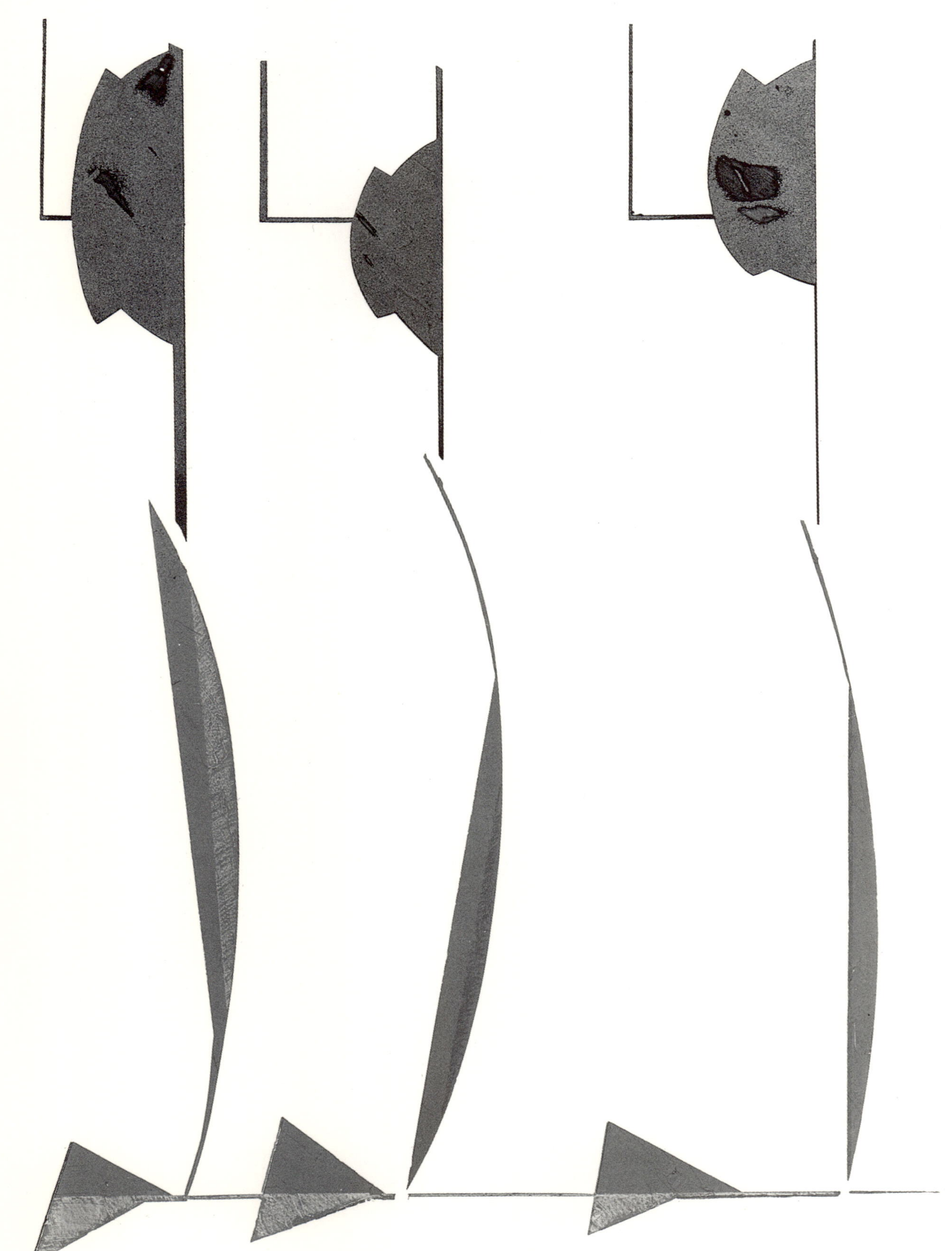

A

12   Unnamed drawing
Acrylic and graphite on paper
76 × 56

13   Razor Drawing   1989
Modelling paste, watercolour, paper collage and walnut shell on paper
76 × 55

14   Razor Drawing   1989
Modelling paste, graphite and walnut shell on paper
90 × 63

15   Razor Drawing   1989
Modelling paste, walnut shell and paper collage on paper
76 × 56

16   Razor Drawing   1989
Modelling paste and walnut shell on paper
76 × 56

17   Razor Drawing   1989
Modelling paste, walnut shell and paper collage on paper
76 × 56

18   Razor Drawing   1989
Modelling paste, graphite, watercolour, paper collage and walnut shell on paper
76 × 56

19   Unnamed drawing
Acrylic, graphite and walnut shell on paper
76 × 56

20   Ties of Blood (Primo Levi Suite)   1986
Relief etching on paper
99 × 69

21   The Most Travelled Road (Primo Levi Suite)   1986
Relief etching on paper
99 × 69

22   Unnamed drawing
Acrylic, graphite and walnut shell on paper
76 × 56

23   Unnamed drawing
Acrylic and graphite on paper
76 × 56

B

24   Unnamed drawing
      Acrylic and graphite on paper
      76 × 56

25   Unnamed drawing
      Acrylic, graphite and walnut shell on paper
      76 × 56

26   Unnamed drawing
      Acrylic and graphite on paper
      76 × 56

27   Mythic Offering   1989
      Acrylic, glass, modelling paste, oak wood, maple wood and aggregate on
      canvas
      244 × 153 × 5

28   Bookburner II   1989
      Acrylic, sand, modelling paste and maple wood on canvas
      248 × 56 × 6

29   Bookburner III   1989
      Acrylic, modelling paste and oak wood on canvas
      214 × 54

30   Bookburner I   1989
      Acrylic, glass, sand and modelling paste on canvas
      270 × 92 × 5

31   Ascent/Descent   1989
      Acrylic, glass, sand, modelling paste, oak wood and maple wood on canvas
      122 × 153 × 5

PLATES

1   Dialogue   1989
      Acrylic, glass, sand, modelling paste and cherry wood on canvas
      244 × 153 × 5

2   Spinoza's Window   1989
      Acrylic, glass, sand, modelling paste, maple wood, marante wood and cherry
      wood on canvas
      126 × 229 × 5

3   Blood Libel   1989
      Acrylic, glass, sand, aggregate, modelling paste and maple wood on canvas
      207 × 275 × 5

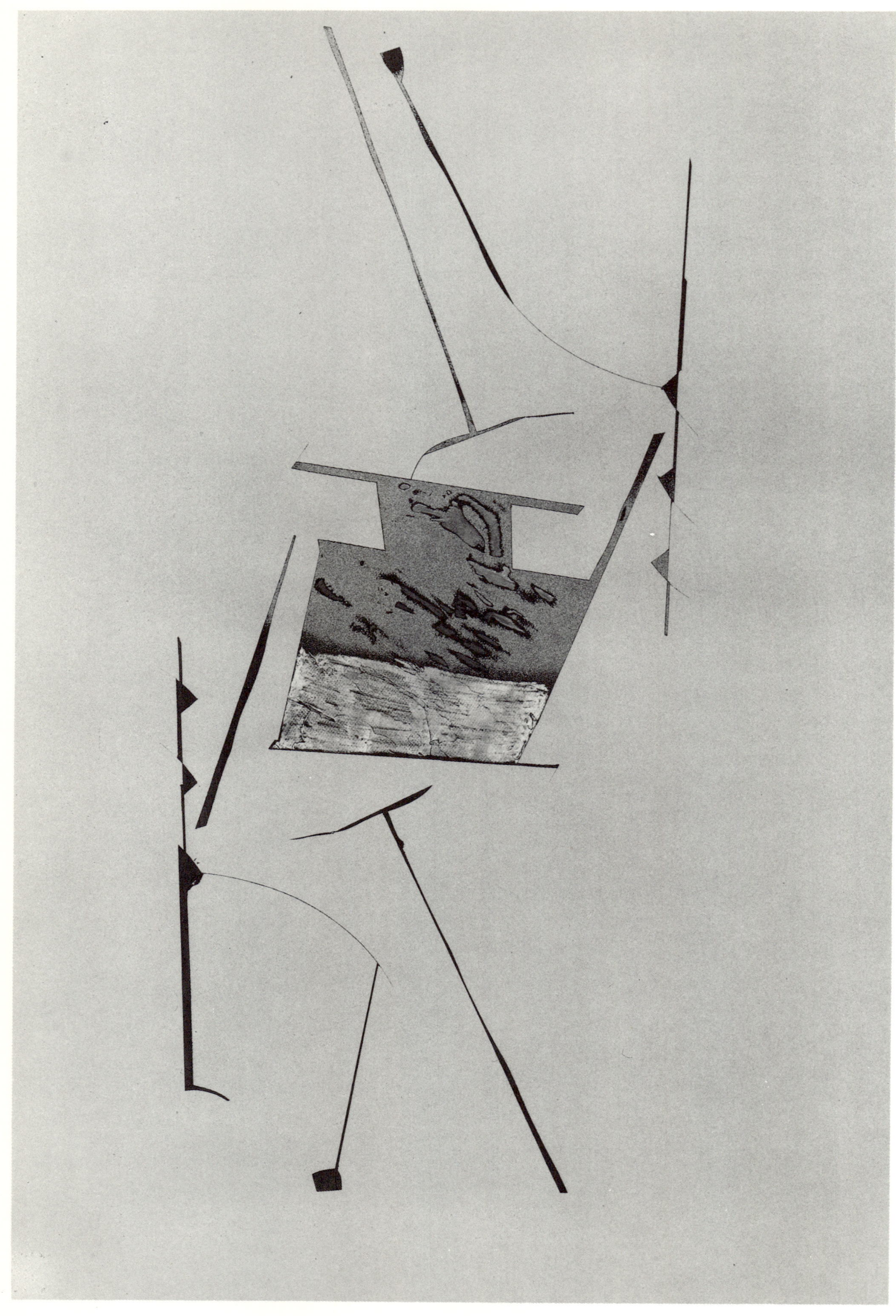

C

4   Passage   1989
Acrylic, aggregate, teak wood, oak wood, glass and modelling paste on
canvas
127 × 77 × 6

5   Ploughshare I   1989
Acrylic, glass, sand, modelling paste and teak wood on canvas
127 × 77 × 6

6   Ploughshare II   1989
Acrylic, glass, sand, modelling paste and teak wood on canvas
127 × 77 × 6

7   Ploughshare III   1989
Acrylic, glass, sand, modelling paste and teak wood on canvas
127 × 77 × 6

8   Razor Drawing   1989
Modelling paste, graphite, paper collage and watercolour on paper
91 × 64

9   Stone Oath Arc   1989
Acrylic, glass, sand and modelling paste on canvas
272 × 153 × 14

10   Stone Oath Alarm   1989
Acrylic, glass, sand and modelling paste on canvas
214 × 122 × 11

11   Stone Oath Danger   1989
Acrylic, glass, sand, modelling paste and aggregate on canvas
214 × 122 × 11

12   Stone Oath Chimney   1989
Acrylic, glass, sand, modelling paste and aggregate on canvas
214 × 121 × 11

13   Stone Oath Burning   1989
Acrylic, glass, sand and aggregate on canvas
275 × 153 × 13

14   Stone Oath Altar   1989
Acrylic, glass, sand and modelling paste on canvas
254 × 254 × 13

15   Unnamed sculpture in maquette form
Oak wood, modelling paste and graphite
92 × 17 × 5

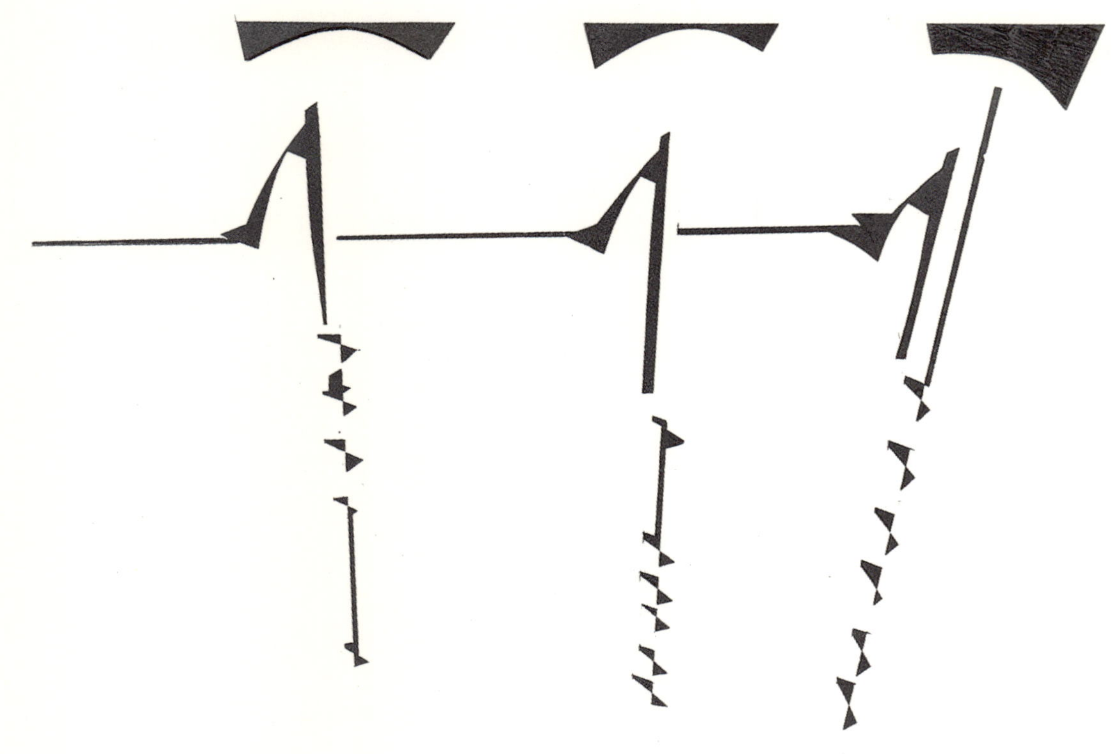

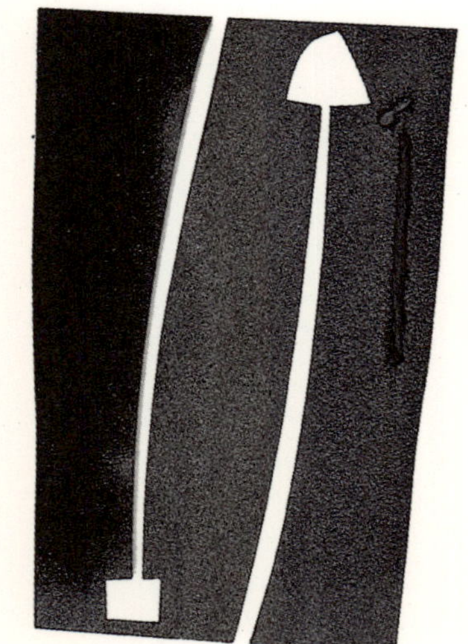

D

16   Unnamed sculpture in maquette form
Oak wood, modelling paste and graphite
97 × 33 × 22

17   Unnamed sculpture in maquette form
Oak wood, modelling paste, graphite and pencil
65 × 23 × 6

18   Raised House   1988
Modelling paste and oak wood
58 × 14 × 6

19   House of Janus   1988
Modelling paste and oak wood
68 × 23 × 6

20   Group of Houses   1988
Modelling paste and oak wood
Various

21   What is to be Remembered   1987
Acrylic, walnut wood, oak wood and light reflective spheres on canvas
120 × 195 × 11

22   Three Houses   1989
Modelling paste and oak wood
52 × 52 × 5

23   Fires in the Night   1988
Acrylic, glass, sand, modelling paste, aggregate and oak wood on canvas
183 × 122 × 6

24   Shelter I   1989
Acrylic, glass, modelling paste, cherry wood and pine wood on canvas
221 × 214 × 8

25   Shelter II   1989
Acrylic, glass, modelling paste and maple wood on canvas
220 × 215 × 7

26   Tabernacle   1989
Acrylic, glass, sand, modelling paste, cherry wood and pine wood on canvas
221 × 214 × 8

27   Freud and Jung   1989
Acrylic, aggregate, sand, glass and teak wood on canvas
294 × 131 × 6

E

28   Proto-Tina   1989
Acrylic, modelling paste, maple wood, glass and aggregate on canvas
244 × 153 × 5

29   Tina I   1989
Acrylic, glass, sand, modelling paste, oak wood and maple wood on canvas
244 × 153 × 5

30   Tina II   1989
Acrylic, glass, sand, modelling paste and oak wood on canvas
254 × 153 × 5

31   Funnel   1989
Acrylic, glass, sand, modelling paste, walnut shell and cherry wood on canvas
275 × 138 × 7

32   Alchemy I   1989
Acrylic, glass, sand, modelling paste and maple wood on canvas
153 × 107 × 5

33   Crucible   1989
Acrylic, glass, sand, modelling paste and maple wood on canvas
187 × 122 × 6

34   Alchemy Lintel   1988
Acrylic, glass, sand, modelling paste, coloured pencil and oak wood on
canvas
119 × 120 × 11

35   Alchemic Lake   1989
Acrylic, glass, sand, modelling paste, maple wood and oak wood on canvas
244 × 153 × 5

36   Divining Rod   1989
Acrylic, glass, sand, modelling paste and oak wood on canvas
244 × 153 × 5

37   Calling Tower   1989
Acrylic, modelling paste, oak wood and marante wood on canvas
244 × 153 × 5

38   Metronome   1990
Acrylic, modelling paste, sand, glass and padauk wood on canvas
189 × 115 × 10

39   Transpositions   1990
Acrylic, glass, modelling paste, sand and padauk wood on canvas
190 × 114 × 5

40   Gnomon Altar I   1981
Acrylic, glass, modelling paste, aggregate and maple wood on canvas
150 × 137 × 6

41   Gnomon Altar II   1989
Acrylic, glass, modelling paste and mahogany on canvas
224 × 124 × 9

42   Gnomon Offering   1982
Acrylic, glass, sand, aggregate and maple wood on canvas
219 × 122 × 5

43   Triptych First Subject   1989
Acrylic, glass, sand, modelling paste and maple wood on canvas
211 × 122 × 5

44   Triptych Second Subject   1989
Acrylic, glass, sand, modelling paste and oak wood on canvas
199 × 122 × 4

45   Triptych Third Subject   1989
Acrylic, glass, sand, modelling paste and oak wood on canvas
199 × 122 × 4

46   The Messiah Myth   1989
Acrylic, glass, sand, modelling paste and teak wood on canvas
204 × 204 × 5

47   Phoenix   1990
Acrylic, modelling paste, glass, sand, padauk wood and zebra wood on
canvas
198 × 168 × 5

48   Diaspora   1990
Acrylic, modelling paste, padauk wood, glass and sand on canvas
229 × 137 × 6

49   Timekeeper (1 of Triptych)   1990
Acrylic, modelling paste, sand and glass on canvas
229 × 121 × 4

50   Crucible II   1990
Acrylic, modelling paste, sand, glass, zebra wood and purple heart wood on
canvas

51   Pax   1990
Acrylic, modelling paste, padauk wood, purple heart wood, glass and sand
on canvas
137 × 198 × 4.5

A   Razor Drawing   1989
Modelling paste, walnut shell and paper collage on paper
76 × 56

B   Razor Drawing   1989
Modelling paste, graphite, watercolour and walnut shell on paper
75 × 55

C   Razor Drawing   1989
Modelling paste, graphite, paper collage and walnut shell on paper
109 × 75

D   Razor Drawing 1989
Modelling paste, paper collage and walnut shell on paper
76 × 56

E   Razor Drawing   1989
Modelling paste and walnut shell on paper
76 × 58